X

NATIONAL
GEOGRAPHIC
KIDS

EXTREME WEATHER

SURVIVING TORNADOES, SANDSTORMS, HAILSTORMS, BLIZZARDS, HURRICANES, AND MORE!

THOMAS M. KOSTIGEN

NATIONAL GEOGRAPHIC
WASHINGTON, D.C.

PUBLISHED BY THE NATIONAL GEOGRAPHIC SOCIETY

Gary E. Knell, *President and Chief Executive Officer*
John M. Fahey, *Chairman of the Board*
Declan Moore, *Executive Vice President; President,
    Publishing and Travel*
Melina Gerosa Bellows, *Publisher and Chief Creative
    Officer, Books, Kids, and Family*

PREPARED BY THE BOOK DIVISION

Hector Sierra, *Senior Vice President
    and General Manager*
Nancy Laties Feresten, *Senior Vice President,
    Kids Publishing and Media*
Jennifer Emmett, *Vice President, Editorial Director,
    Kids Books*
Eva Absher-Schantz, *Design Director,
    Kids Publishing and Media*
Jay Sumner, *Director of Photography, Kids Publishing*
R. Gary Colbert, *Production Director*
Jennifer A. Thornton, *Director of
    Managing Editorial*

STAFF FOR THIS BOOK

Erica Green, *Senior Editor and Project Editor*
James Hiscott, Jr., *Art Director/Designer*
Lori Epstein, *Senior Photo Editor*
Miriam Stein, *Photo Editor*
Paige Towler, *Editorial Assistant*
Allie Allen, Sanjida Rashid, *Design Production
    Assistants*
Margaret Leist, *Photo Assistant*
Carl Mehler, *Director of Maps*
Grace Hill, *Associate Managing Editor*
Mike O'Connor, *Production Editor*
Lewis R. Bassford, *Production Manager*
Susan Borke, *Legal and Business Affairs*

PRODUCTION SERVICES

Phillip L. Schlosser, *Senior Vice President*
Chris Brown, *Vice President, NG Book Manufacturing*
George Bounelis, *Senior Production Manager*
Robert L. Barr, *Manager*
Haley Harrington, *Imaging Technician*

The National Geographic Society is one of the
world's largest nonprofit scientific
and educational organizations.
Founded in 1888 to "increase and dif-
fuse geographic knowledge," the
Society's mission is to inspire people
to care about the planet. It reaches more than 400
million people worldwide each month through its
official journal, *National Geographic*, and other mag-
azines; National Geographic Channel; television
documentaries; music; radio; films; books; DVDs;
maps; exhibitions; live events; school publishing
programs; interactive media; and merchandise.
National Geographic has funded more than 10,000
scientific research, conservation, and exploration
projects and supports an education program pro-
moting geographic literacy.

For more information, please visit national
geographic.com, call 1-800-NGS LINE (647-5463),
or write to the following address:

National Geographic Society
1145 17th Street N.W.
Washington, D.C. 20036-4688 U.S.A.

Visit us online at nationalgeographic.com/books

For librarians and teachers: ngchildrensbooks.org

More for kids from National Geographic:
kids.nationalgeographic.com

For information about special discounts for bulk
purchases, please contact National Geographic
Books Special Sales: ngspecsales@ngs.org

For rights or permissions inquiries, please contact
National Geographic Books Subsidiary Rights:
ngbookrights@ngs.org

Trade paperback ISBN: 978-1-4263-1811-5
Reinforced library edition ISBN: 978-1-4263-1812-2

Printed in the United States of America
14/WOR/1

*The publisher gratefully acknowledges Jack Williams
and Michelle Harris for their expert reviews of the book.*

CONTENTS

INTRODUCTION

AS A JOURNALIST, I have traveled all around the world, exploring the environment from the Arctic Circle to the Amazon rain forest to the deserts of the Middle East and Africa to remote islands in the Pacific Ocean. There is one thing all of these places have in common: extreme weather. But guess what? You are likely experiencing extreme weather wherever you live, too. I wrote this book to help you understand why the weather is changing and what you can do to stay safe when it does.

In this book, we'll look at weather, which is what's happening in our atmosphere with pressure, heat, cold, wind, and moisture. We'll also look at climate, which is the pattern of weather over a long period of time. And we'll talk about how global warming is making our climate change. When global temperatures rise and warm the planet, the weather changes. It is because of this rise that we see more heat waves, droughts, and wildfires. The change in temperatures also affects thunderstorms and rain patterns and the way the wind blows. As Earth tries to balance these warm temperatures, some parts of the planet can get really cold as well. Seems crazy, right? Well, it is. The science behind extreme weather and climate change can be complicated.

To try to sum it up simply: The overall temperature of our planet depends on how much heat is absorbed from the sun and how much Earth sends as energy back into space. If all the sun's rays returned to outer space, Earth would be too cold a place for us to live. Certain gases in Earth's atmosphere absorb the heat of the sun and keep it here. Those gases are called greenhouse gases. Greenhouse gases have always been released by most living things such as plants, trees when they die, animals, humans as they breathe out, and even nonliving things such as volcanic eruptions. But scientists are convinced that we humans are creating additional greenhouse gas from pollution, such as the exhaust fumes from cars and the smoke from chimneys. These extra gases heat the planet up, too, which causes changes of all kinds in the environment and the weather.

Today we are seeing parts of the world that once experienced droughts get flooded, and areas that were once very hot are colder. Scientists are studying these environmental changes to find out what is causing them. Most scientists agree that we are affecting climate change with the pollution we are putting in the air.

Meanwhile, we have to live with extreme weather. So what to do? Aha! That is what this book explains.

Hopefully you will use this book to understand why the weather is changing and what you can do to prepare for it. Another important part of this book is safety. After all, it's one thing to learn why the weather is getting extreme, but it's another to actually know what to do when extreme weather strikes. You'll find out what to do in all types of circumstances: when it gets really hot or really cold; when there are droughts, floods, or wildfires; when a tornado hits or a thunderstorm begins; or when a blizzard comes and there are whiteouts. You'll even see what you can do after a storm passes and the weather goes back to normal. I've tried to give you both the knowledge and the tools you'll need when the weather turns against you. It is my hope that you won't just read this book, but that you'll also use the tips from this book if you are ever caught in extreme weather.

Thomas M. Kostigen

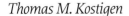

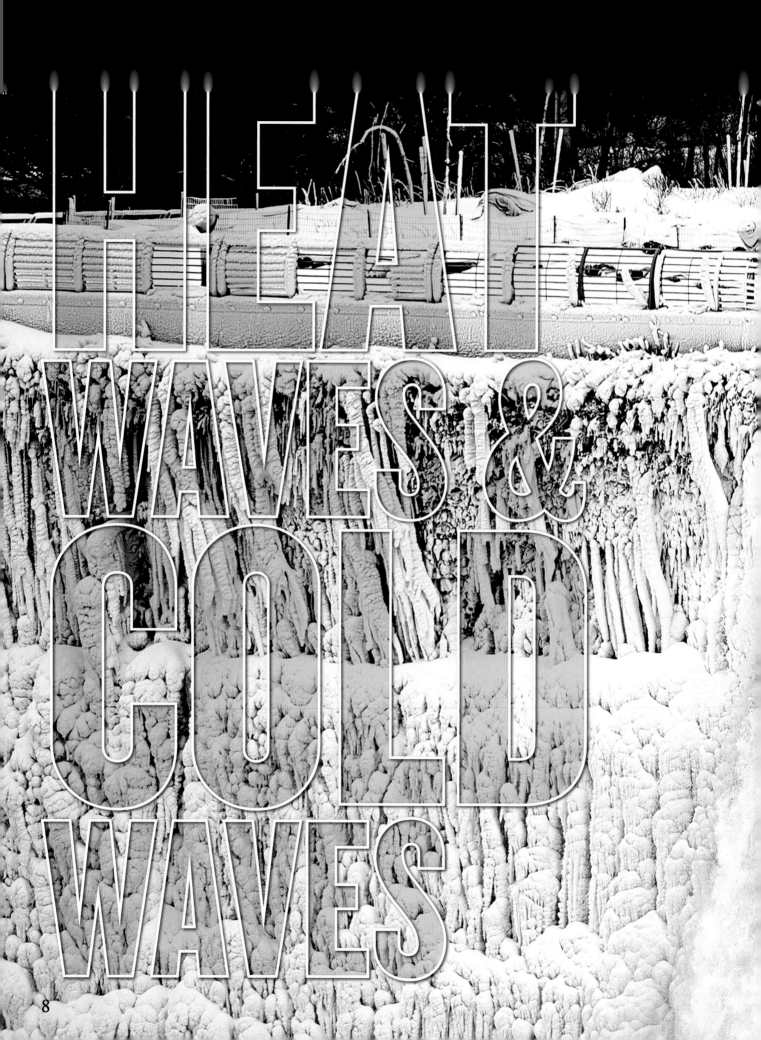

HEAT WAVES & COLD WAVES

CHAPTER 1

Niagara Falls / 2014

HEAT WAVES

[When SUPER-hot temperatures and often humidity rise to above average for two or more days]

YOU KNOW WHAT IT'S LIKE when you're taking a shower and the water gets so hot it feels like it's burning your skin? Or when the oven door opens and that whoosh of hot air hits you in the face? A heat wave can feel similar to that!

Unlike with a snowstorm, a rainstorm, or a tornado, you don't see a heat wave; you feel it. And you may feel it for a while. If it stays abnormally and uncomfortably hot for more than two days, it's a heat wave. Heat waves can be very dangerous. Hot temperatures can lead to many heat-related illnesses. When you get sick from extreme heat, it's called

hyperthermia. Hyperthermia is when your body's internal temperature gets too hot, just like when you have a fever. Of course, heat waves can do more than make you sick. They can lead to conditions that set the stage for wildfires, droughts, dust storms, and all sorts of other problems for the planet.

An interesting thing to keep in mind about heat waves is that every person feels and experiences heat in different ways. How you are affected by heat depends on your age, your health, and also where you live. If you live in Hawaii and you are used to the weather being warm all the time, then it might not seem so hot when the temperature is 86°F (30°C). But if you are from Alaska, where the weather is almost always cold, then 86°F (30°C) might make it seem like Earth is burning up.

Take the famous heat wave of 2003. This heat wave was one of the worst in history because temperatures rose so high and stayed high for so long in areas that are usually cooler. In Europe, temperatures stayed above 100°F (37.8°C) for more than a week! Many older people who didn't have

NATURE'S SIGNAL

WANT TO KNOW HOW HOT IT IS OUTSIDE? Listen to a cricket! By counting the number of times a cricket chirps, you can calculate the temperature. Here's how: Count the number of times a cricket chirps every 14 seconds, add 40 to that number, and the total is the temperature in Fahrenheit. Take a few measurements and then use the average to determine the temperature.

air-conditioning and couldn't move to somewhere cool became sick and died. The heat didn't affect only people. It was so hot that crops shriveled, rivers dried up, and grapes turned to raisins on the vine.

A few severe heat waves struck the United States in 2012. The entire country saw its average temperature rise. In some places, temperatures reached 100°F (37.8°C) for days. People who lived in the middle of the United States, in places such as Detroit, Michigan, and Chicago, Illinois, experienced the highest temperatures. Still, it was scorching hot almost everywhere. In fact, it was so warm that people in New Hampshire were able to go to the beach at a time when they normally snow ski!

No matter where you live, though, you are probably experiencing warmer air temperatures and more heat waves than your parents did at your age.

Hundreds try to stay cool floating in the water during a heat wave in China, 2013.

HOW & WHERE DO HEAT WAVES BEGIN?

Heat travels north and south, away from the Equator. Wind carries heat, but when the wind dies down, hot air gets trapped and stays in one place. If it stays there for more than two days, it's a heat wave!

CANADA

UNITED STATES

MEXICO

TRAPPED HEAT BECOMES A HEAT WAVE

eXpert Tips

THE AMERICAN SOCIETY FOR THE PREVENTION OF CRUELTY TO ANIMALS (ASPCA) offers tips for taking care of pets during a heat wave. On a warm day, a parked car can become as hot as a furnace. Even when the windows are open, the temperature inside the car can become dangerous. Never leave your pet alone in a parked vehicle. When indoors, make sure he or she has plenty of clean and fresh water. Limit their exercise to early mornings or later in the evening when it is cooler. Always check the sidewalk or road during hot days with your own hand before you take your pet for a walk. If it is too hot to touch, it could burn your pet's paw pads. Always keep an eye on them in case they overheat. If you notice they start to pant a lot, have difficulty breathing, drool excessively, or vomit, it may be a sign that they are sick and you need to contact your veterinarian.

BEFORE
A HEAT WAVE YOU SHOULD:

HAVE AN ADULT HELP YOU:

- Get to know your neighbors, especially those who are sick or elderly. The sick and elderly can suffer the most from heat waves because their bodies may not be strong enough to fight heat sickness.
- Make an emergency kit that includes drinking water, canned foods (like beans, vegetables, and soups), a can opener, flashlights, and a portable radio.
- Turn your refrigerator and freezer to their coldest settings. They will keep things cooler longer if the power goes out. (Don't keep opening and closing the refrigerator or freezer door; this lets cold air out and heat in.)

DURING
A HEAT WAVE YOU SHOULD:

- Stay indoors.
- Wear loose-fitting and light-colored clothes.
- Drink lots of fluids.

AFTER
A HEAT WAVE YOU SHOULD:

- Have an adult check on any elderly or sick neighbors to make sure they are feeling okay.
- Check on your pets.
- Be sure to wear sunscreen if you go outside.
- Continue to drink lots of fluids.

Czech Republic / 2013

13

Surface temperatures all over the world have been rising. Scientists say it is going to keep getting warmer. That's why it is important to learn what you can do to cool down when it gets hot.

It is not just daytime temperatures that have gotten hotter either; nighttime temperatures have risen, too. When it stays hot at night, it is harder for people to cool off. Over the course of a few days, this increases the risk of heat-related complications. So, the next time a heat wave strikes, use your gadgets, tips, and smarts to stay cool!

It can get so **hot** during a heat wave that train tracks **bend.** When the temperature hits **95°F** (35°C), railroad workers often go looking for **bends** or buckles in tracks so trains can keep **running** on schedule.

Gadgets

A HANDHELD FAN is useful during a heat wave. Some come with misters that can spray you with water, others are powered by the sun (solar-powered), and other fans come inside helmets or baseball caps so you don't have to carry them—you can wear them! All of them are designed to blow air onto and around your body in order to lower your body temperature, which will keep you from getting sick.

HOW TO MAKE YOUR OWN
REHYDRATION FLUID

Sometimes if you sweat a lot and you don't drink enough water, your body goes out of balance. You get sick because you lose important minerals your body needs to function. These minerals are called electrolytes, and they help keep just the right amount of water in your body so you can function and feel well. Without these minerals, you might start to vomit or get diarrhea.* Some sports drinks have electrolytes in them to make you feel better. But instead of buying sports drinks, you can make your own rehydration fluid at home!

1/2 teaspoon salt
6 teaspoons sugar
1 liter water (at room temperature)

Blend it all together. Drink in small amounts (by the spoonful) every few minutes for a few hours or until you feel better.

***Remember:** Heat stroke can be very serious. On a hot day, if someone's skin is hot and dry and their heart is beating fast, they may need medical attention. Also, if you are not feeling well, tell an adult and talk to your doctor.*

WHY IS IT GETTING HOTTER?

GLOBAL WARMING IS MAKING EARTH HOT. Global warming, an increase in temperatures around the planet, happens when certain types of gases trap the sun's heat and keep it from escaping into space. Pollution caused by humans creates more of these gases, which traps more heat.

Children cool off in a fountain in London, England.

15

COLD WAVES

[When temperatures drop WAY below average and stay low for more than 24 hours]

SCIENTISTS IN ANTARCTICA know about cold. At a research station near the South Pole, they recorded a temperature of minus 128.6°F (-89.2°C). At that temperature, if you were to wash your hair and go outside, it would freeze on end. Your spit would turn to ice. And if your skin was exposed to air, you would be in serious danger of immediately suffering from frostbite! Frostbite—when your skin freezes—can be dangerous, even deadly.

Okay, so an average cold wave isn't that extreme, but it can still be dangerous. Hypothermia is when your body temperature drops and you become ill.

During this kind of cold sickness, your teeth may start to chatter or your body may shiver. If this happens, get someplace warm quickly. Your body is telling you that it is too cold! Because cold weather can be so dangerous, it's important to learn what cold waves are and how to bundle up and prepare for dealing with these extreme cold temperatures.

We tend to experience colder temperatures after the sun sets. It also gets cold in places covered in light or white surfaces, such as those covered in snow and ice or the sands of a desert. Light-colored surfaces act like trampolines for the sun's rays. When the rays hit these surfaces, they bounce right back into outer space. Because the rays are not absorbed, these areas don't keep warm for very long. This, plus seasonal changes, like the very little sunlight at the Poles in the winter, means it stays cold in the polar region.

A trio of Adélie penguins nestle on the ice in Antarctica.

NATURE'S SIGNAL

IF YOU FIND SPIDERWEBS inside your house, it means it may get cold soon. Spiders go indoors to seek shelter when the weather is cool. Black widow spiders especially don't like low temperatures, so look out for them in your home's dark corners, basements, and closets!

Our planet is also cooled by wind. Winds carry cold air from the Poles to other parts of the planet. Winds are caused because there is a difference in temperatures between the polar regions and the area around the Equator. You may have heard of the jet stream, a band of winds and air currents that circles the globe. When these wind streams stretch below the Arctic Circle and pressures change, this can cause cold snaps or wet winters, depending on where you live.

Scientists say the Arctic jet stream that blows all that cold air may be dipping farther south than it has in years past. That is why, these same scientists say, people living in Canada, northern Europe, and the northern United States have seen their winters become especially cold, or filled with more cold waves.

But cold snaps are not just recent events. During the War of 1812, France's first emperor, Napoléon Bonaparte, invaded Russia. By the time he reached Moscow, it was winter, and it got so cold that his army had to retreat.

Morning commuters in Toronto, Ontario, Canada, make their way to work during a deep freeze, with temperatures feeling like minus 40°F (-40°C) in January 2014.

BEFORE
A COLD WAVE YOU SHOULD:

- Make sure you have enough winter clothing and blankets to keep you warm.
- Plan to bring your pets inside or plan to keep them warm. Make sure there is a fresh supply of water for them that won't freeze.
- With a parent, check that your home heaters are a distance away from anything that could catch fire (like curtains, clothes, paper, or blankets).

DURING
A COLD WAVE YOU SHOULD:

- Stay indoors or find warm shelter.
- Try not to talk or sing outside. Cold air can hurt your lungs and throat.
- Keep active by walking or playing lightly. Don't move around so much that you sweat, but move enough to keep your blood flowing. This will make you warmer.

AFTER
A COLD WAVE YOU SHOULD:

- Get out of any wet clothing and dry off as fast as possible if you've been out in the cold.
- Slowly warm your core, your biggest body parts (your chest and stomach), first. Then warm your extremities (your arms and legs, fingers and toes) to avoid shock.

19

This eventually caused him to lose the war. One hundred years later, in 1912, a cold wave in the United States brought many of the lowest temperatures ever recorded. In the state of Maryland, the temperature dropped to minus 40°F (-40°C), a state record that remains in place today. In 2012, another cold wave hit many parts of the world. It felt like the North Pole had moved to Europe!

Wind, freezing temperatures, ice, and snow are all things a cold wave can bring. But don't worry, not every cold wave is dangerously frigid. And there are lots of ways you can stay safe and warm when wicked winter weather comes your way.

Niagara Falls / 1920

A blast of cold air barreled down from the Arctic and blew through North America in January 2014, making temperatures feel like minus 60°F (-51.1°C). It was so cold in some places that the temperature was lower than it was at the South Pole!

People walk in a park covered with frost on December 22, 2013, in Czech Republic.

Gadgets

YOUR HANDS AND FEET are the first parts of your body to get cold. If you know that temperatures are going to get really, really cold, it may be smart to use hand and feet warmers. These are sometimes called "mitten warmers" or "toe warmers" and usually come in small packets that you pop into your hand or place under your feet. The packets contain either powder or liquid, and when you shake them or snap them, they create a chemical reaction that makes heat. There are other types of warmers that you can heat in the microwave.

HOW TO DRESS IN LAYERS TO

STAY WARM

To stay warm, you need to stay dry. That means you have to keep checking to make sure you aren't sweating. The wetness from sweat makes your body lose the heat it needs to keep you warm. This is why you should dress in layers. Wearing three layers is the best way to stay warm. The first layer of clothing you should put on is called a base layer. It should be something lightweight, like long underwear. The middle layer of clothing should be your really warm layer, like a sweater or fleece. And your last layer of clothing should be something waterproof and/or windproof, like a rain jacket or parka.

WHY IS IT GETTING COLDER?

OUR CLIMATE IS CHANGING because of global warming. Global warming affects Earth by making the weather act differently over long periods of time. The average temperature for the entire planet is warmer now than in the past, but some places, like the North and South Poles, still remain quite cold. Global warming also adds energy to some storms, making them stronger. And on occasion, stronger-than-usual winds bring very cold air to places that typically have warm winters. So global warming is causing both hotter and colder weather.

DROUGHTS, WILDFIRES & SAND- STORMS

A monstrous dust storm threatens Phoenix, Arizona, U.S.A.

CHAPTER 2

DROUGHTS

[A period of time when the lack of water or moisture impacts people, animals, and plants]

A DROUGHT HAPPENS WHEN there isn't enough water for plants and animals, including humans, to survive and thrive. People need water to live. Without water, we cannot survive for more than a few days. When it doesn't rain for a long period of time, or when lakes, rivers, and streams (the places where we get most of our fresh water) don't carry enough water to us, it causes a drought.

We not only need water to drink, we need water to grow and raise our food so we can eat, too. You might think the oceans have plenty of water, but that is saltwater. We need fresh water to survive.

Goat herders / Ethiopia

We mostly get fresh water from rain or when snow and ice on mountaintops melt to fill lakes and rivers.

Less than one percent of all the water on Earth is fresh water. One percent is a tiny amount. (Think of it as the size of one of your teeth compared to your whole body; that's not very much!) Actually, there is more fresh water on the planet, only we can't access it because it is frozen as ice inside a glacier or too deep underground.

NATURE'S SIGNAL

THE SNOWPACK is all the snow and ice on the ground that melts by summer. A thin snowpack in winter is a sign that a summer drought is likely. Winter snow melts and ice melts are what refill rivers, lakes, and other sources of fresh water that we tap for our everyday use. So in the winter, when there is less snow on the ground and less ice on mountaintops, there will be less water during the spring and summer.

Areas at Risk of DESERTIFICATION

NORTH AMERICA

EUROPE

ASIA

AFRICA

EQUATOR

SOUTH AMERICA

AUSTRALIA

DRY LANDS (DESERTS AND AREAS AT GREATEST RISK OF DESERTIFICATION)
Extremely dry/desert
Other dry land areas

ANTARCTICA

Surprisingly, the same amount of water is on the planet now as was during the time of dinosaurs. Today, because the number of people on the planet keeps growing, we need more water both for drinking and for food production. Seventy percent of the fresh water we use is for agriculture. With temperatures and our global population rising, we are slurping up more water.

The way it rains is changing, too. Instead of rain coming in even, steady streams, the way water flows out of your shower, it now comes down in buckets more often than it used to. Scientists are convinced that there will continue to be more intense rainstorms because of the warmer air, which can hold more water. So now, when storms happen, the amount of rain often increases. These intense storms with bursts of rain mean plants and soil don't have enough time to sponge up all that water and it ends up getting washed away before it has a chance to do its job of helping grow food.

One of the most famous droughts, called the Dust Bowl, lasted for nearly ten years—

Xeriscape

BEFORE
A DROUGHT YOU SHOULD:

- Check around your house for leaks and any dripping faucets. One drip a second wastes 2,700 gallons (10,220 L) of water per year. That's probably enough to fill every bathtub in your neighborhood!
- Talk to your parents about xeriscaping (ZEAR-ah-SKAY-ping). It may be difficult to pronounce, but it means planting vegetation that doesn't need a lot of water (think cactus plants). You can also xeriscape by using stones and wood chips in place of grass. Obviously you don't need to water stones or wood chips.
- Never waste water. That means don't let the faucet run too long or spend a long time in the shower. Conserve whenever possible.

DURING
A DROUGHT YOU SHOULD:

- Never let the tap run to get cool water. Instead, keep your drinking water in the refrigerator. Nor should you let the tap run to get hot water for cooking or drinking. Instead, heat it on the stove or in a microwave.
- Only flush the toilet when needed. It wastes water if you use your toilet instead of a trash can for paper products, bugs, or other types of waste.

AFTER
A DROUGHT YOU SHOULD:

- Continue to conserve water wherever and however you can. Remember that droughts can return.
- Try not to take baths. They can use three times as much water as the average-length shower. And when you do take a shower, take a short one!
- Never let the water run as you brush your teeth or wash your face. This just wastes water down the drain.

eXpert Tips

ACCORDING TO THE U.S. FEDERAL EMERGENCY MANAGEMENT AGENCY (FEMA) AND THE AMERICAN RED CROSS:
"A normally active person needs to drink at least two quarts [1.9 L] of water each day." When it's hot and humid, you need even more. And if your area might suffer from power outages that cut your water supply, don't forget that you also need water to make food and to wash things, including your body. If you need to store water, store at least one gallon (3.8 L) per person for each day. Try to keep a two-week supply.

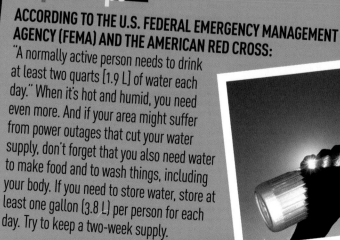

from 1931 to 1939. It affected mostly the middle of the United States, where a lot of food is grown and livestock is raised. At that time, farmers had been abusing the land by overplowing, and so when a really long period of dry weather came along, the ground crumbled and the rich layer of topsoil blew away. All that dirt was swept into the wind and created huge dust storms called "black blizzards" or "black rollers."

More recently, in Australia, the same thing happened. In 1995, it rained very little—a lot less than usual—and the dry weather continued until 2012! That's 17 years! That drought was called the Millennium Drought.

Droughts occur all over the world, so it's important to conserve water no matter where you live to ensure that we will have enough for the future.

Our planet has become so dry that water **poaching** has become a big problem. Several years ago, countries in Asia tried to **make** a deal with the United States to ship away water from the **Great Lakes.** U.S. and Canadian authorities have since made it **illegal** to take and ship any water from the Great Lakes.

A gigantic dust cloud / Oklahoma, U.S.A., 1935

Gadgets

ONE OF THE FIRST STEPS IN CONSERVING WATER is knowing how much you use. This isn't always easy. To find out, you have to find the water meter in your home and then calculate how much water was used over the course of, say, a month. Then you have to divide that amount by how many people live in your house. And then you have to do even more math to estimate how much each person used per day. Even then there is no way to calculate how much water your shower uses versus, say, your bathroom sink. Enter technology. Indoor water monitors can show your water usage by faucet or appliance. These are little computer screens that you install in your home to show how much water you are using. They also can alert you when your home springs a leak! The more you know about how much water you use, the more you can save.

HOW TO INSTALL A
RAIN BARREL

Rain barrels help save water for nonrainy days. They usually have three parts to them: a top hole, an upper drain, and a lower drain. Have an adult help you buy a rain barrel. These look like big trash barrels with holes on the top that are covered by screens. This lets the rainwater in. On the bottom is a faucet. You can attach this to your garden hose. Keep the bottom faucet in the closed position until you want to use it to water the lawn or the garden. After it rains, try it! Clean water should flow.

Scientists generally agree that climate change will cause wet areas of the world to get wetter and dry areas to get drier.

WILDFIRES

[A fire located in a forest, field, or wildlands with the potential to burn quickly, spread fast, or get out of control]

IT'S EASY TO IMAGINE A FOREST FIRE, with trees burning, flames, and lots of smoke filling the air. But it's hard to imagine the size of wildfires. They are often huge—easily stretching to the size of a whole neighborhood or much larger!

Fire can travel fast, and it can jump. When a fire jumps, it is called spotting. That's when sparks or embers fly through the air with the help of wind. These fire specks can land miles away and start another fire there.

NATURE'S SIGNAL

IF YOU SEE OR SMELL SMOKE during the day, or see a red or an orange glow at night, a fire may be nearby. If you hear crackling or see sparks, check to see if you need to evacuate!

FIREFIGHTERS often drop something called slurry from aircraft to fight fires. Slurry is a mixture of water and fertilizer that sticks to trees and other vegetation and helps put out flames. It also will help plants regrow once the fire is extinguished.

What do wildfires have to do with weather, you might wonder? They mostly occur when the weather is dry and tree branches and leaves have dried out, too, making them flammable. In the United States, wildfire season begins in the spring, when the weather usually begins to heat up after a colder winter season. Then, it extends into the summer and fall after there have been long periods of dry and hot weather.

Wildfires are caused by many things. They can begin when lightning from a thunderstorm strikes the ground and trees catch fire or when lava spews from a volcano. Of course, they can also begin if the temperature gets so hot that it causes something to catch fire from all that heat. Humans also start fires. Campfires, sparks from engines, matches, and tossed cigarettes can all ignite fires that can burn out of control. Out-of-control fires are not good for the planet, nor for us. Getting caught in a wildfire is very dangerous. People can be harmed by a wildfire's heat, flames, and smoke (not to mention wildfires can damage property).

Even though there have been wildfires on our planet for hundreds of millions of years, they may be happening more often and growing bigger now than they have ever been. Our warming climate may be leading to the dry conditions that then lead to more fires.

The Rim Fire / California, U.S.A., 2013

Yosemite National Park / California, U.S.A.

People watch a wildfire by a beach in Sydney, Australia, 2013.

BEFORE
A WILDFIRE YOU SHOULD:

- Check that your garden hose can reach every area of your house. Inspect the trees and shrubs in your yard and ask an adult to trim them if they are too close to your house. If there are dead leaves or tree branches on the ground, sweep them away.
- Test the smoke alarms in your house every month.

DURING
A WILDFIRE YOU SHOULD:

- Follow police and emergency services evacuation procedures.
- Leave your house immediately if you are told to do so.
- Go to an evacuation spot if you are outside. If there isn't one, look for a low-lying area that is clear of debris and vegetation.
- Shut all the windows, vents, and doors in your house to stop drafts and to help prevent flames from getting into your home if you are stuck inside.

AFTER
A WILDFIRE YOU SHOULD:

- Keep watch for a few hours after the fire has passed, checking for smoke or other signs it might have returned.
- Stay away from any pits of ash.
- Take care of your pets until all the ash has been cleared and the fire has been fully extinguished.

eXpert Tips

HOW TO HELP AN ADULT BUILD A CAMPFIRE:

The United States Forest Service's Smokey Bear says that if you are building a campfire, be careful where you pick your spot. Make sure fires are allowed, then choose a spot that is downwind and is at least 15 feet (4.6 m) from your tent and gear. Next, make a 10-foot-diameter (3-m) clearing around the spot you chose. Remove grass, twigs, and firewood. Also, make sure there aren't any tree limbs or flammable objects nearby. Then dig a hole in the dirt about 1 foot (0.3 m) deep. Surround the pit with rocks. Now your fire pit is ready. Fill it with small pieces of wood. (Place any unused wood upwind and away from the fire. And keep a bucket of water and a shovel close by in case the fire needs to be put out quickly.) After an adult lights the fire, remember to tell him or her to keep it under control. To extinguish the fire, allow the wood to burn to ash and pour water on it. Work with an adult to shovel and mix the ashes and embers with the water until everything is wet and cold.

33

As we live, work, and play in forested areas, there is also a greater chance for fires to start by accident.

Some of the biggest forest fires have been in the United States. But China, Russia, Canada, and Australia have had some of the worst wildfires. In 2010, during a heat wave in Russia, several hundred wildfires burned, destroying land and producing heavy smog over the cities—even miles away from the fires. Many people died in these historic fires, which is why we have to learn how to prevent wildfires and how to stay safe when one is near.

Did you know that trees always naturally produce electricity? There is so much power running through certain big trees, such as oak, that firefighters use them as a power source when they want to monitor a fire. Firefighters attach sensors with rechargeable batteries to the trees—the batteries recharge using energy from the tree!

Gadgets

SPARKS FROM MOTORBIKES, LAWN MOWERS, or anything else that has an engine—large or small—can cause a wildfire. That's why it's important to use spark arrestors. Ask your parents to get them and put them on anything that has an engine. These gadgets prevent sparks from escaping and causing fires.

HOW TO EXTINGUISH FLAMES IF YOU
CATCH FIRE

There are three words to remember if you have caught fire: *stop*, *drop*, and *roll*.

STOP means just that. Do not run away; it will only make the fire worse. **DROP** means lower yourself to the ground. Also, try to protect your face with your hands. **ROLL** means to turn yourself over and over (rolling) on your side until the flames are smothered and gone.

If you see someone else catch fire, be careful not to catch fire yourself. Tell that person to stop, drop, and roll!

STOP

DROP

ROLL

"We're seeing bigger fires today. And once they get going, they're burning for a longer time. They're also burning across a wider area."
—Ecology professor Steve Running

SAND STORMS

[Sand and sand particles blown into the air by high winds, creating a storm]

WHAT IF YOU TOOK A HANDFUL OF DIRT and tossed it into the air but it didn't fall to the ground? Imagine the wind carrying it higher into the sky. That's what happens during a dust storm or a sandstorm. But instead of just a handful of dirt or sand blowing through the air—there are massive storms of sand! Sandstorms and dust storms can get so big that they block out the sun. They can even swallow up entire cities.

These types of storms usually happen in deserts, because there is so much dry sand on the ground. Big sandstorms like these are called haboobs, a word that comes from the Arabic word *haab*, which means "wind" or "blow." The Arabic word is used because these kinds of storms usually occur in African deserts, such as the Sahara, where many people speak Arabic. But they don't happen only there.

In 2011, a massive haboob nearly 100 miles (160 km) wide and 1 mile (1.6 km) high blew through the state of Arizona in the United States and covered the city of Phoenix in sand and dust. The dust and sand blew so

NATURE'S SIGNAL

PINECONES ARE ONE way to tell if there is going to be dry weather. Pinecones open their scales when the weather gets extremely dry. They do this to scatter their seeds. When the air is moist, they close up to keep their seeds dry.

Pine seeds are transported by the wind, so they have to stay as dry and as light as possible in order to fly. Dust and sand, of course, travel in much the same way. So if a pinecone's scales are open, be on the lookout for dry weather.

A sandstorm at Lake Banzena, Mali

high into the air that airplanes had to be rerouted. (Pilots couldn't see through a sandstorm like that!)

These giant dust storms and sandstorms are caused by winds and dry weather. As temperatures rise, the ground becomes drier and dustier, and since extreme storms are occurring more often, sandstorms also are happening with more frequency.

Monsoons occur when the wind changes direction during a particular time of the year. It's these wind changes that often cause dust storms and sandstorms. In the southwest part of the United States—in states such as Arizona, New Mexico, and Texas—the monsoon season is during summer. In places such as India, the dry monsoon season occurs during winter.

Of course, dust storms and sandstorms have been occurring throughout history. And more than one dust storm or sandstorm can kick up at the same time. One Sunday, in the U.S. states of Oklahoma and Texas during the 1935 Dust Bowl, huge, dark clouds of dust and sand blew all around.

Anatomy of a MONSOON

CUMULUS CLOUD

DOWNDRAFT

UPDRAFT

DOWNPOUR

HABOOB

An intense downward current of air ahead of the storm can cause a haboob.

Dust Bowl / Pratt, Kansas, U.S.A., 1937

Cracked earth / Kenya

BEFORE
A SANDSTORM YOU SHOULD:

- Get indoors as soon as possible and don't take any chances of being caught outside.
- Communicate with your family, friends, and neighbors to let them know where you are.
- Have a cloth handy to cover your nose and mouth in case you need to evacuate while sand and dust are flying through the air.

DURING
A SANDSTORM YOU SHOULD:

- Stay indoors.
- If you must go outside, do not walk near roads or in places where there is traffic of any sort; drivers blinded by the storm won't be able to see you.
- Use a moist cloth to cover your nose and mouth, both indoors and outdoors. Breathe through it.

AFTER
A SANDSTORM YOU SHOULD:

- Be aware that winds may pick back up again; so be sure the storm has passed before you risk going outside.
- Use caution walking on sidewalks and pathways; sand can make surfaces slippery.
- Try to avoid breathing the outdoor air for hours after a storm passes; the lingering dust can still be harmful to your lungs.

eXpert Tips

ACCORDING TO THE NATIONAL PARK SERVICE, YOU should stay on marked paths when you tour a park or go hiking. Also, consider not going four-wheeling or riding ATVs in the desert. Disturbing the ground soil is a leading cause of dust storms and sandstorms. When you go off-trail, delicate habitats and vegetation can be destroyed. This makes soil weaker and gives the wind a chance to sweep loose dirt up into the air.

A man rides a horse during a sandstorm in Bredjing, Chad, 2007.

They covered everything they came in contact with in a thick coat of dark dirt. The day was called Black Sunday.

In ancient times, in 525 BC, a sandstorm whipped up so much sand in the Egyptian desert that it buried hundreds or maybe even thousands of soldiers who were marching there. In 2009, Italian researchers found some of the remains of the buried soldiers.

Even if you aren't marching through the desert, you should still take precautions during dry, hot weather and be on the lookout for dust storms or sandstorms!

Gadgets

DID YOU KNOW THAT YOU CAN GET YOUR OWN PERSONAL DUST MONITOR? These devices analyze the air you are breathing and alert you when dust levels get too high and become dangerous. Miners use these frequently to ensure that they are breathing healthy air deep underground in the mines where they work. But if you live in the desert, or in a place where dust storms and sandstorms occur regularly, getting your own dust monitor may be something you and your family will want to do.

Great Sand Sea / Egypt

HOW TO TIE A MILITARY-STYLE
HEAD SCARF

This head wrap, called a *shemagh*, *kaffiyeh*, or *ghutrah*, is a scarf-like wrap that is made to protect you from the sun and to protect your mouth, nose, and eyes from blowing dust and sand. Here is how you wrap one.

• START WITH A LARGE SCARF or a piece of material about 42 inches by 42 inches (1 m by 1 m). (A bandanna is too small.) Open it so that it is in a full square. Fold it in half to form a triangle.

• CHOOSE A POINT THREE-QUARTERS OF THE WAY along the folded edge and hold it to your forehead. Let the rest of the scarf drape over the back of your head. • Take the shorter end of the fold and PULL IT UNDER YOUR CHIN and up toward the back of your head. • Take the longer side and PULL IT ACROSS YOUR FACE, leaving only space for your eyes. • Then WRAP THE LONGER PIECE UP OVER YOUR HEAD toward the other side and tie the two ends together.

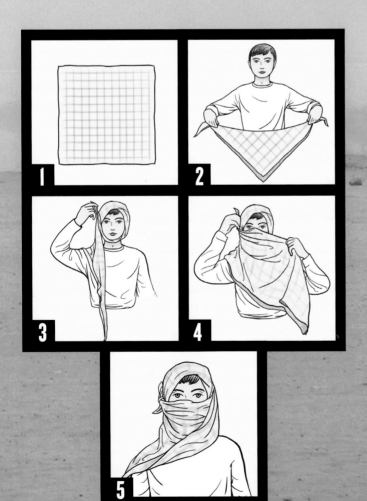

A sandstorm / Bahai, Chad

BLIZZARDS, WHITEOUTS & ICE STORMS

Ice storm near
Lake Geneva,
Wisconsin, U.S.A.,
2005

CHAPTER 3

BLIZZARDS

[Snowfall and high, fast-blowing winds (over 35 miles an hour/56.3 kph) that last for more than three hours]

YOU DON'T WANT TO BE OUTSIDE during a blizzard. It's cold. It's snowy. And the wind blows so hard that snowflakes can feel like pellets hitting you in the face. For a snowstorm to turn into a blizzard, the wind has to be blowing really fast—a speed of at least 35 miles an hour (56.3 kph). In a blizzard, there is so much snow falling or blowing around that it blocks your vision. Blizzards last at least three hours and occur most often not on mountains but on open plains.

Canada, the upper parts of the United States, and northern Europe get lots of blizzards because cold air

NATURE'S SIGNAL

BEFORE A STORM, horses and cattle will herd together. They tend to stay off hills and head for lower ground, such as valleys. Horses will often put their heads down and point their rears toward the storm's direction. So, if it seems like a storm is coming, take a look at a horse's butt to find out what direction the storm is headed.

ARCTIC AIR MOVES SOUTH

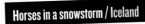

CANADA
U.S.
Arctic Air

P L A I N S

Direction of Storm

MIDWEST

NORTHEAST

Cold Front

WINTER jet stream patterns that dip far south over the United States (large blue area, above) are likely to stir up blizzards across the Plains and Midwest into the Northeast.

45

from the Arctic, the region around the globe that stretches roughly 1,635 miles (2,631 km) south from the North Pole, blows down and mixes with the warmer, moist air coming up from the Equator.

The worst blizzard ever witnessed was in Iran in 1972. There, near the northwest border with Turkey, 26 feet (8 m) of snow fell. That is about three times as high as a ceiling in the average room. The snowfall lasted nearly a week and covered 200 towns!

In 1993, the blizzard known as the "Storm of the Century" dropped so much snow across the United States that nearly half the people in the country got caught in the storm! The electricity went out for millions of people, and snowdrifts as high as 30 to 40 feet (9–12 m) were created in cities. In some cases, it took days to clear pathways and roads and to dig out cars.

Emperor penguins / Antarctica

Blizzard of 1888 / New York City

Shoveling cars out of the snow / New York City, 1993

Municipal workers spread salt on the streets of Madrid, Spain, after a snowstorm in 2009.

BEFORE
A BLIZZARD YOU SHOULD:

- Work with an adult to make a blizzard emergency kit with rock salt to melt ice on walkways, sand to improve traction, snow shovels, and blankets.
- Turn water taps open slightly so they drip and pipes won't freeze. Also, open kitchen cabinet doors beneath the sink to let warm air reach the plumbing.
- Find a warm place to wait out the storm.

DURING
A BLIZZARD YOU SHOULD:

- Stay indoors until you know the snowstorm has stopped and then venture out only if necessary.
- Walk carefully on snowy, icy walkways if you must go outside.
- Keep dry. Remember: Wet clothing makes you colder.

AFTER
A BLIZZARD YOU SHOULD:

- Shovel out walkways and driveways as soon as you can to expose the ground to sunlight to keep ice from forming.
- Use salt to help prevent ice, and throw sand on the ground to keep from slipping.
- Be on the lookout for black ice that is hard to see and can cause you to fall.

Gadgets

DID YOU KNOW THAT THERE IS A SPECIAL RADIO network for weather reports from the National Weather Service in the United States? It's called NOAA Weather Radio All Hazards. You can buy a special receiver that alerts you when there is a weather event in your area. Some of these come with rechargeable batteries, so you don't have to worry about getting new ones. Others can be powered by hand cranks or the sun (that's called solar power!). Some have all three options—and a built-in flashlight, too—just in case the electricity goes out.

In Antarctica, blizzards can bring winds that top 100 miles an hour (160 kph). There, the snow can fall so hard that sometimes you cannot see your hand even if it is right in front of your face.

In January 2014, a bulge in polar vortex winds, which normally circle the Arctic, pushed far south into North America with bitter-cold air that helped stir up major storms east of the Rockies. Some climate scientists believe global warming could have caused this by making the polar jet stream weaker, which made it more curvy, so it dipped south. Scientists predict there are going to be even more blizzards all around the world, because with global warming, the air holds more moisture, which leads to heavier snowfalls.

The word "blizzard" wasn't used to describe the weather until after the U.S. Civil War. Until then, "blizzard" was used to describe musket fire and cannon fire and as a way to describe a series of punches thrown by professional boxers.

Digging out the entrance to a tent during a blizzard in Chile

eXpert Tips

THE UNITED STATES SEARCH AND RESCUE TASK FORCE SAYS: If you get caught outside during a blizzard, find shelter to stay dry and cover all exposed parts of your body. Build a lean-to, windbreak, or snow cave for protection from the wind. Build a fire for heat and to attract attention. Place rocks around the fire to absorb and reflect heat. And if you get thirsty, do not eat snow. It lowers your body temperature. This can make you very sick. Instead, melt snow first, then drink it.

HOW TO SIGNAL FOR HELP DURING A
SNOWSTORM

IF YOU ARE IN A CAR, hang a rag, plastic bag, or piece of cloth from a window or antennae as a distress signal. IF YOU ARE ON FOOT, stomp out an **X** or the word **HELP** or **SOS** in BIG LETTERS in the snow and place rocks or tree limbs in the impressions. Because trees and rocks are dark, they will stand out in the white snow and allow rescuers to spot you from above.

According to **Paul Kocin** of the National Weather Service, **while there may be fewer blizzards throughout the year, changing global weather patterns have contributed to larger, fiercer storms that result in heavier snow.**

WHITEOUTS

OUTS

[Snow falling or blowing so hard that it makes it difficult to see anything in front of or around you]

YOU ALWAYS HEAR "Don't stare directly at the sun." That's because it can blind you. Well, a whiteout can, too. The reason everything looks so white has a lot to do with the sun. Even when it is a cloudy day, the sun's rays are out. These rays are reflected on white things, like snow. This attraction makes a snowy day really, really bright. It also makes everything look the same—the falling snow, the sky, and the ground all become white. And when everything looks the same and snow swirls around in front of us, we can see only whiteness. Of course, this means we have trouble figuring out where things are.

Whiteouts can happen in a number of ways. Often they occur when there is heavy snowfall and so much snow in the air that it blocks our ability to see. Another way is when snow on the ground gets blown back up into the air by wind and blocks our view. We also get whiteouts when snow and ice are on the ground. In this condition, light reflects off the snow and ice and everything looks the same. That's when it's hard to see any difference between the ground and the sky. Whiteouts happen most often in the spring and autumn, when the sun is closer to the

Polar bears / Churchill, Canada

NATURE'S SIGNAL

IF IT STARTS TO GET REALLY WINDY at the same time that it is snowing, it may be nature's way of warning you that a whiteout could be on its way.

A woman braves blizzard conditions in Anchorage, Alaska, U.S.A.

horizon. They can be very dangerous. People driving cars can get into accidents. Airplane pilots can lose their sense of direction. It can be risky just being outside or walking down the street. Some people have gotten lost during a whiteout in their own front yards!

Scientists note that the number of whiteouts will likely increase because climate change will lead to more heavy snowfalls. But there have been many well-known whiteouts in the past.

One of the worst whiteouts in history happened during the Children's Blizzard of 1888. A snowstorm began covering most of the central United States just as school was letting out and as students were walking home. Hundreds of children were caught outside in the whiteout and many died. The storm became infamous and the story of how the children got caught in the storm has been told repeatedly.

SNOW SQUALLS

VERY COLD

COLD

BLINDING WHITEOUT

How a **WHITEOUT** Occurs

WHITEOUT
When snow squalls meet very cold temperatures just above a cold air front, clouds and snow combine, causing blinding whiteouts.

Some animals will stop and stay in one place during a whiteout because, just like humans, they can't see. However, reindeer, polar bears, arctic foxes, and seals can see in a whiteout! They have special vision that allows them to see through whiteout conditions.

Biking in a snowstorm / Wichita, Kansas, U.S.A., 2014

BEFORE
A WHITEOUT YOU SHOULD:

- Listen to and watch weather reports to find out how bad the storm is getting. If the weather looks like it is getting worse and the wind and snow are blowing hard, find somewhere safe and warm inside.
- If you are outside, look around to see how far in front of you it is possible for you to see. If it's not too white yet, find a safe place you can get to—fast.
- Then, check around for something you recognize to get your bearings.

DURING
A WHITEOUT YOU SHOULD:

- Stay where you are. Because you won't able to see well, you can easily get lost.
- Signal for help if you got lost in the storm.

AFTER
A WHITEOUT YOU SHOULD:

- Wait until it's clear enough for you to see well before you go anywhere.
- If you remained outside, head for the nearest home or shelter where you can ask for help.
- Be careful about where you walk. Slippery snow and ice may have blown around or formed during the whiteout.
- Do not try to walk far. Go to the nearest place that looks like it would be safe shelter. Sometimes things look closer in the snow than they really are.

eXpert Tips

PROFESSIONAL MOUNTAINEERS SAY: If you get caught in a whiteout, stay put. It may seem like a bad idea to stand still in the wind and cold, but it's more dangerous to keep walking when you cannot see. To buffer the wind, dig a small pit in the snow and sit in it with your back to the wind. Or, if there are rocks around, pile them up and hunker down on the leeward, or downwind, side of them. Pile the rocks between you and the direction the wind is blowing. Keep watching for the whiteout to clear. You want to be able to see a few feet in front of you before you start walking again, so wait out the storm until you can. Try to remain calm rather than panicking or walking in circles.

It is used as a reminder to keep students safe during winter.

Still, some of the worst whiteouts occur in Antarctica, which surrounds the South Pole and is almost completely covered by miles-deep ice. In 1960, one blizzard there caused whiteout conditions that lasted for days! No matter how long or short a whiteout, it can be dangerous. Learn what to do to stay safe.

Whiteouts can make you **dizzy.** Because your **vision** is linked to your sense of balance, when you can't see as well, you can't **balance** as well. And when you can't balance as well, you can sometimes feel dizzy and fall down, or feel **sick.**

Children's Blizzard / U.S.A., 1888

Gadgets

TO BE PREPARED FOR WHITEOUT CONDITIONS, you should get a pair of goggles. Unlike most sunglasses, goggles are designed to protect the area surrounding your eyes, including the sides. They can help you see better in whiteouts because they not only block snow from blowing in your eyes, but some also come with colored lenses that allow you to judge distance better. Experts say you should wear light-colored lenses in orange (amber), yellow, rose, or blue during whiteouts.

54

WHITEOUT

If you get lost in a whiteout, you should be prepared to signal rescuers. Here are some simple signs you can leave in the snow with branches or dark objects so rescuers can see the signal from the air.

LL — **ALL IS WELL**

JL — **I DON'T UNDERSTAND**

→ — **I WILL GO THIS WAY**

I — **I NEED A DOCTOR**

II — **I NEED MEDICAL SUPPLIES**

▷ — **SAFE TO LAND**

X — **I CANNOT PROCEED**

K — **TELL ME WHICH WAY TO GO**

F — **NEED FOOD AND WATER**

Even though an area might receive snow less often than it did in the past, the amount of snowfall it sees might increase because of the growing severity of snowstorms.

ICE STORMS

[When rain pelts down and freezes to ice]

LET'S FOLLOW THE PATH OF A DROP in an ice storm. Near the top of a cloud, with rising air holding it up, is one tiny ball of ice. But soon other balls of ice stick to it; it becomes too heavy for the air to hold it up. This ball begins to fall as a lumpy snow crystal. After a while, it falls into air that's warmer than 32°F (0°C) and melts into a raindrop. Then it falls into a layer of air that's colder than 32°F (0°C), but it doesn't freeze even though it's only 25°F (-3.9°C). Instead it is "super cooled."

Finally this drop hits a rough piece of tree bark and instantly turns into ice. Thousands of supercooled water drops hit the tree. This is all part of an ice storm. Of course the temperature near the ground must be 32°F (0°C) or below for water to freeze. When lots of raindrops hit the ground and turn to ice, it creates an ice storm.

It doesn't take a lot of ice on the ground to cause an ice storm; just a small bit of ice on the ground can be really dangerous. Ice makes things very heavy.

NATURE'S SIGNAL

DURING THE WINTER, ladybugs find protection from the weather by clustering together and living under leaves or bark. In many U.S. states, some species of ladybugs have found a warm place to spend winter—human homes! If you spot one or a whole group of them swarming in your house, chances are that winter is coming.

Even a small amount of ice can cause trees to fall over, can put so much weight on power lines that they break and cut off the electricity to your home, and can topple telephone poles. Also, of course, ice makes roads and sidewalks extremely slippery.

In 1998, the Great Ice Storm hit Canada and parts of New England and New York in the United States. It seemed like ice blanketed everything. The storm caused the electricity to go out for millions, leaving them in the dark during the intensely cold weather. Because of the storm, people died. The event was so scary that many people bought T-shirts saying, "I Survived the Great Ice Storm." How did it happen? Warm air carrying a huge amount of water vapor traveled all the way up from the Gulf of Mexico to the Great Lakes, where it moved over cold air near the ground, causing freezing rain and sleet—tiny frozen water drops—and ice started pelting down.

A frozen transit stop / Bulgaria

Great Ice Storm / Canada, 1998

BEFORE
AN ICE STORM YOU SHOULD:

- Gather rock salt to melt ice on walkways.

DURING
AN ICE STORM YOU SHOULD:

- Shut all the windows and doors and make sure the heat is on to stay warm indoors.
- Make sure you wear waterproof clothes on top of your warm clothes if you have to go outside. And wear shoes that have thick treads. If you have crampons, or athletic shoes with cleats, wear those.
- Watch your step! There may be black ice that you cannot see on the ground, and you can easily slip and fall.

AFTER
AN ICE STORM YOU SHOULD:

- Stay away from power lines that have fallen down. These lines are really dangerous because they can still have electricity going through them that can hurt or kill you.
- Look up to be aware of tree limbs that could fall.
- Look down, look for ice, and walk slowly. Just because the ice storm is over doesn't mean the ice is gone.

eXpert Tips

EMERGENCY MEDICAL PROFESSIONALS say to never touch anyone being electrocuted, or you could be electrocuted yourself. You should find an adult to call for help. If there aren't any adults around, call for help on the telephone. Do not use objects such as brooms or sticks to move the person or the source of electricity (like a fallen power line). Stay far away from the area. You can get electrocuted even by being close to the problem.

59

In 2007, an ice storm hit North America, stretching from southeastern Canada to Texas in the United States. In many places, thick layers of ice formed on the ground and a lot of damage was done to homes, buildings, and businesses. Thousands of people had to leave their homes and find safety at shelters. Even the trains were shut down.

Scientists who study climate change say that because of the increased moisture in the air, our storms are getting stronger. With stronger storms, we're more likely to see conditions like those that lead to ice storms.

Did you know there is such a thing as **black ice?** Black ice is extremely dangerous on roads and walkways because these surfaces look **clear** but are actually **glazed** with super-slippery ice. You just can't see it.

Gadgets

IF YOU GET CAUGHT IN AN ICE STORM, there is a good chance the electricity will go out in your neighborhood. Ice on power lines weighs wires down, causing them to break. So be ready. Sure a flashlight can help you see in the dark, but why not use a headlamp? That way you can keep your hands free for balance or to shovel if you have to go outside. Indoors, keeping your hands free also means you can help with safety chores more easily.

HOW TO BEST MELT ICE ON THE
GROUND

To melt ice on the ground, you need to be able to see it. That means shovel off any snow first. (Be careful not to slip while doing this.) Next, chip away as much ice as possible with your shovel. Then, sprinkle salt crystals in rows on the ground. Start at the center and work out to the sides. Remember: You don't need to use a lot of salt. Salt can harm plants. Ask an adult to help you find some eco-friendly alternatives to salt, like alfalfa meal.

Salt **SMARTS**

1 Shovel first

2 Sprinkle salt

3 Read label and use sparingly

Strong polar vortex winds circle the Arctic, bottling up cold air. A big temperature difference between the Arctic and places to the south makes the vortex strong. But as the Arctic warms, the vortex weakens, sometimes sending bitter-cold air to the south.

THUNDER-STORMS & MUD-SLIDES

A man's path is blocked by a 20-mile (32-km) landslide in the Karmadon Gorge, North Ossetia, Russia.

CHAPTER 4

THUNDER-STORMS

[A storm with thunder, lightning, and (usually) heavy rain]

LET'S SAY IT'S NIGHTTIME and you are in bed. A flash of light comes through your window. All of a sudden you hear a loud *boom!* You know the sound is coming from outside, but the noise is so loud it sounds like it is everywhere all at once—maybe even directly over your house. Then it starts to rain really, really hard. It can be scary, but it's just a thunderstorm.

Thunderstorms are the most common type of storm on Earth. The loud booms they make are called thunderclaps. The flashes of light are called lightning. Thunderstorms often produce heavy rain, and even giant hailstones. Hail refers to balls of ice that form in

Hailstones

thunderstorms. Most are small, maybe the size of a pea. But some are larger, even as big as a softball.

Every minute, about 2,000 thunderstorms are raining down somewhere on Earth. Thunderstorms are most common in the spring and summer months, during the afternoon and evening hours, when surface air temperatures have heated up.

Thunderstorms can happen in winter, too. These unusual storms produce snow instead of rain—thundersnow!

Thunderstorms are made of "cells." They begin when water vapor in rising, warm, humid air begins condensing into cloud drops that form a tall, lumpy "cumulus" cloud—this is the storm's "cumulus" stage. As the cloud grows, ice crystals form and begin falling, dragging air down with them. This is the thunderstorm's "mature" stage with both rising air (updrafts) and sinking air (downdrafts). This is when a thunderstorm produces heavy rain, hail, lightning, and downdraft winds that can blast down to the ground with 100-mile-an-hour-plus (160-kph-plus) speeds. Fortunately, these are rare. Eventually, warm

Swarm of midges / Uganda

NATURE'S SIGNAL

KEEP AN EYE ON THE CLOCK. Then look for bugs. Up to 12 hours before a thunderstorm, black flies and mosquitoes might swarm. Then, about an hour before the storm hits, they disappear. These bugs like humidity, which is water or moisture in the air. But, like humans, they don't like getting too wet and take cover from all the rain a thunderstorm causes. So before it rains, flies and mosquitoes hide.

air stops rising into the cell, the downdrafts weaken, and the rain or hail lets up. This is the "dissipating" stage.

While many thunderstorms live and die as a single cell, thunderstorms with more than one cell, or "multicell cluster thunderstorms," are much more common. They can produce huge amounts of rain, which can, among other things, lead to floods. In these clusters, new cells form as older ones die. The biggest type of thunderstorm is a "supercell." These long-lasting storms are awesome in size and power and can produce tornadoes and giant hailstones. They are more powerful than some of the most destructive weapons on Earth!

Because thunderstorms happen so frequently, there are new examples every year of just how much destruction they can cause. In 2013, a huge supercell caused a massively destructive tornado that blew through the U.S. state of Oklahoma. It created wind speeds close to 300 miles an hour (483 kph). That is faster than a race car!

Tornado / Iowa, U.S.A., 2004

Tornado damage / Oklahoma, U.S.A., 2013

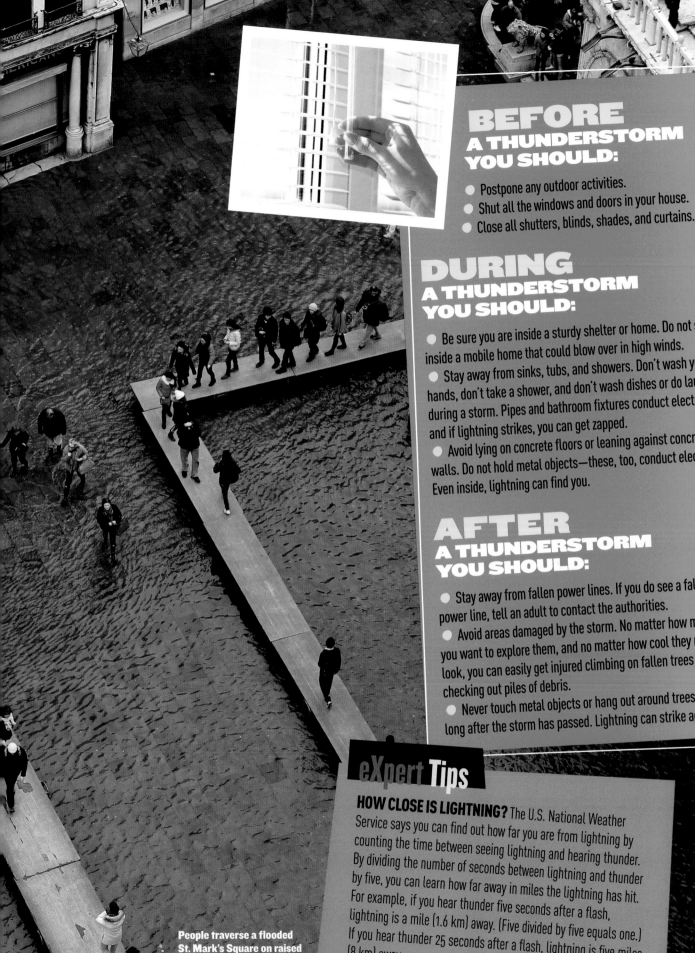

BEFORE
A THUNDERSTORM YOU SHOULD:

- Postpone any outdoor activities.
- Shut all the windows and doors in your house.
- Close all shutters, blinds, shades, and curtains.

DURING
A THUNDERSTORM YOU SHOULD:

- Be sure you are inside a sturdy shelter or home. Do not stay inside a mobile home that could blow over in high winds.
- Stay away from sinks, tubs, and showers. Don't wash your hands, don't take a shower, and don't wash dishes or do laundry during a storm. Pipes and bathroom fixtures conduct electricity, and if lightning strikes, you can get zapped.
- Avoid lying on concrete floors or leaning against concrete walls. Do not hold metal objects—these, too, conduct electricity. Even inside, lightning can find you.

AFTER
A THUNDERSTORM YOU SHOULD:

- Stay away from fallen power lines. If you do see a fallen power line, tell an adult to contact the authorities.
- Avoid areas damaged by the storm. No matter how much you want to explore them, and no matter how cool they might look, you can easily get injured climbing on fallen trees and checking out piles of debris.
- Never touch metal objects or hang out around trees until long after the storm has passed. Lightning can strike again.

eXpert Tips

HOW CLOSE IS LIGHTNING? The U.S. National Weather Service says you can find out how far you are from lightning by counting the time between seeing lightning and hearing thunder. By dividing the number of seconds between lightning and thunder by five, you can learn how far away in miles the lightning has hit. For example, if you hear thunder five seconds after a flash, lightning is a mile (1.6 km) away. (Five divided by five equals one.) If you hear thunder 25 seconds after a flash, lightning is five miles (8 km) away.

People traverse a flooded St. Mark's Square on raised walkways in Venice, Italy.

The most damage ever caused by a thunderstorm was due to a storm that produced softball-size hailstones that came down in Dallas and Forth Worth, Texas, U.S.A., in 1995. Many people were gathered together celebrating at an outdoor festival when the hail began to fall. Imagine being outside when softballs starting falling from the sky. People had to run to get indoors. But not everyone was able to find shelter, and more than 400 people were injured—many of them parents who used their own bodies to shield their children from the falling chunks of ice.

Of course, thunderstorms happen in most of the world but are very rare in the Arctic and have never been reported in Antarctica. They are most common in the tropics, but those storms are generally weaker than the ones in the North American Great Plains.

Because temperatures around the world keep getting higher, some climate scientists say that even though there are already millions of thunder-storms every year, there will be even more to come.

When thunder **roars**, go **indoors**.

Gadgets

LIGHTNING RODS CAN HELP save you and everyone in your house from getting electrocuted. If a lightning rod is affixed to the top of your house, the lightning will be attracted to that and not your roof!

Ask your parents about getting a lightning rod system. Trained professionals will have to install it, but it will be fun to watch them and learn about what they are doing.

WHAT TO DO IF LIGHTNING
STRIKES

The National Weather Service and other lightning safety experts say the number one lightning safety rule is "When thunder roars, go indoors." Stay inside until 30 minutes after thunder stops. Indoors means inside a large building with electrical wiring and plumbing. If lightning hits the building, its electricity is likely to follow wires or plumbing to the ground. A second best choice is to head inside a vehicle with a metal roof and with the windows rolled up. Forget anything you might have heard about squatting on your heels if lightning seems to be near. If lightning hits nearby, the electricity could spread out over the ground and run up one of your legs.

You should keep track of the weather if you're going to be outdoors. Before going out, check to see whether thunderstorms are predicted.

BE EARTH FRIENDLY!

USE LESS ELECTRICITY by switching the light off every time you leave a room and by moving your desk next to a window to use natural light instead of a lamp. When you use less electricity, less fuel is required to produce energy, and fewer greenhouse gases are emitted and you'll be able to help fight global warming.

MUDSLIDES

[Wet and massive chunks of earth that slide down the side of a mountain often because of heavy rains]

HAVE YOU EVER STOOD at the top of a waterslide and zoomed down into a pool? A mudslide is just like that, except instead of a kid racing down a slide, there are piles of wet dirt rushing to the bottom of a hill. While that all sounds kinda fun, and a mudslide has a silly-sounding name, mudslides are actually very dangerous weather events.

Mudslides sometimes include larger objects and are then called debris flows, because all sorts of things get swept away by them—cars, large boulders, furniture, even people and pets. A mudslide happens on the top

The remnants of a hill where a massive mudslide took place on March 27, 2014, in Oso, Washington, U.S.A.

layer of soil. Usually we see mudslides after a heavy rain, because the rainwater mixes with the dirt and soil, causing things to slide. Mudslides also happen when soil has been disturbed by a wildfire or humans.

Here's how a slide happens: When water gathers quickly during heavy rain or snowmelt, it forms a slurry. A slurry is any thick mixture of water and another substance, like a paste, that moves. This slurry then flows rapidly, taking with it at avalanche speed whatever is on the top layer of the soil. The sliding slurry can pick up rocks, trees, vehicles, and even entire buildings.

NATURE'S SIGNAL

Sometimes the ground will let you know that a mudslide is on its way. If there are weird bulges in the ground, something may be wrong with what is underneath. Rocks or the layers of soil that support the topsoil may be weak. This can mean the ground is about to give way. Also, cracks may appear in places on the ground where they have never appeared before. If you find water seeping out from these cracks, or puddles, when no source of water is around, these can be warning signs of a mudslide.

71

Mountain, canyon, and coastal areas are most susceptible to slides, especially in areas where the soil has been weakened by fire or human actions. When a fire scorches the earth, it kills plants and vegetation and hardens the soil. This allows water to move much faster over the surface.

One of the most intense debris flows happened in northern India during June 2013. Heavy rains fell onto the Himalaya. These mountains are extremely tall and steep, so the rain had a long way to fall down to the valleys below. Once the mud started sliding, it, too, went for a long, sharp journey down. Entire roads were washed away along with bridges and hundreds of homes.

Also in 2013, there were lots of wildfires in the United States in the state of Colorado.

Colorado, U.S.A. / 2013

A man salvages his belongings from his house in Leh, Jammu and Kashmir, India, following a night of flash floods and mudslides in August 2010.

BEFORE
A MUDSLIDE YOU SHOULD:

● Do some homework! Investigate whether there have ever been debris flows in your area. If they have occurred in the past, they are likely to happen again.
● Plant shrubs or other vegetation around the edges of your lawn to help absorb water.

DURING
A MUDSLIDE YOU SHOULD:

● Stay alert and awake. Listen to NOAA Weather Radio All Hazards (see sidebar p. 47) or a portable, battery-operated radio to learn what is happening in your neighborhood.
● Move quickly. Mudflows can travel faster than you can walk or run, so if one is heading for you, get out of its way.
● If you get caught in a mudflow, look upstream so you can try to stay clear of large objects flowing your way.

AFTER
A MUDSLIDE YOU SHOULD:

● Keep your distance from the disaster area. More slides could come.
● Look and listen for injured and trapped people. Never try to rescue people in the slide area yourself. Instead, find an adult and tell them, or direct rescuers to where there are people who need help.
● Tune in to weather reports in case more rain is predicted. Floods sometimes follow debris flows.

eXpert Tips

REPLANT AFTER A DEBRIS FLOW. The United States Geological Survey says that after a debris flow or landslide, you should replant things as quickly as possible on the damaged ground. Plants can stop soil from eroding and help prevent flash flooding and future slides. Work with your community to come up with a plan for replanting in your area.

Because the ground had dried from the fires and the vegetation that holds water was gone, when rains hit, mudslides came along in force. That summer, a massive mudslide washed away cars and destroyed roads. You could see cars floating down the highway!

Find out if there have been debris flows in your area. If your neighborhood is at risk, work with your community to help plant vegetation that can absorb water and hopefully prevent a mudslide. Of course, also know your evacuation routes and what to do if a mudslide occurs.

In 2005, the **entire** side of a hill **dropped** into the town of La Conchita, California, U.S.A. Ten people died. People were trapped under debris—some for as long as **ten** hours. The whole landslide lasted just **15** seconds. Some claim the slide happened because of **fruit!** They claim the lemon and avocado ranch at the top of the mountain did not have proper **drainage.**

Gadgets

IF THERE IS A MUDSLIDE and you have to step outside, one thing is for sure: You are going to get dirty—muddy actually. That's why you should have a pair of mud boots. Mud boots are rubber boots that are usually knee-high. They will keep your feet and legs dry and can help you walk through the piles of wet dirt and debris that come with a slide. You often see firemen and other emergency responders wearing these types of rubber boots to help them walk through torn-up areas and to protect their feet and legs.

Emergency workers at the site of a landslide at La Conchita, California, U.S.A., 2005

HOW TO POSITION YOUR BODY DURING A LANDSLIDE OR MUDSLIDE

If getting out of the way of a mudslide isn't an option and you get caught in its flow, protecting your torso and head are most important. The best way to do this is to curl into a tight ball. If you can, keep your feet in front of you to protect yourself from crashing into large, stationary objects in your way.

First, place your knees as close to your chest as possible. Then wrap your elbows over your knees and tuck your chin tightly into your chest. Put your hands over your head if possible to stay in this position until the danger passes. As soon as you can, get out of the slide's path.

Heavy rains caused mudslides, destroying many houses and streets in Nova Friburgo, Brazil, 2011.

BE EARTH FRIENDLY!

WHEN IT GETS HOT IN THE SUMMER, use a fan instead of turning on the air conditioner. If you must use the AC, set the thermostat no lower than 78°F (25.5°C) and keep a fan buzzing to stay cool. In the winter, wear more layers of clothing instead of cranking up the heat.

DOWN-POURS & FLOODS

CHAPTER 5

An aerial view of the
flooded River Rhine
in Germany

DOWNPOURS

[Rain that comes down in one heavy stream instead of lots of little raindrops]

BEING IN A DOWNPOUR is a bit like standing under a bucket full of water and having someone dump it over your head.

When rain falls, it does so at different speeds. The largest raindrops, which are 5 millimeters across (about the size of a housefly), fall at roughly 20 miles an hour (32 kph). Tiny drops that are less than 0.5 millimeters across (the size of a grain of salt) fall at about 5 miles an hour (8 kph). For a downpour, you need a cloud with enough moisture to make big raindrops that fall faster.

These days there are more blasts of heavier rainstorms because of an increase in temperatures around the globe. With the rise in global temperatures, more moisture is stored in the air. When conditions

come together for clouds to grow and create precipitation, more moisture is available to fall to earth.

Heavy downpours are dangerous because they can cause floods and mudslides and damage to plants, buildings, and property, not to mention human life. The most amount of rain ever recorded in one hour was in the small town of Holt, Missouri, U.S.A., where, in 1947, an entire foot (0.3 m) of rain fell in less than an hour!

A cyclist is caught in a heavy downpour in Beijing, China, 2012.

NATURE'S SIGNAL

TO FIGURE OUT WHETHER IT IS GOING TO RAIN, look up at the sky. If the sky darkens and there are fluffy, low-lying clouds piled on top of each other, that means rain is likely. Along with these signs, wind from the south that shifts in a counterclockwise direction usually means that it is about to downpour. Or you can listen. Frogs increase their serenading (*ribbits!*) just before a rainstorm. The extra water in the air allows them to stay out of the water longer ... and croak!

The most rain ever recorded in one year was in Cherrapunji, India, between August 1860 and July 1861. More than 1,000 inches (2,540 cm) of rain fell. That is more than 80 feet (24 m) of rain! Imagine an 80-foot-tall (24-m) wave. That's how much water poured down.

Heavy rain in San Miguel, Ecuador

eXpert Tips

PET EXPERTS SAY you should plan for pet safety at the same time you plan for your own safety. This means making sure your pets have a safe and dry place to go during a heavy rainstorm. During the storm, keep a close eye on them and make sure all gates and doors are closed. Make sure your pets are always wearing their identification tags.

BEFORE A DOWNPOUR YOU SHOULD:

- Postpone any outdoor activities.
- Make sure all windows, doors, and seals are closed tight to prevent leaks.
- Listen to local radio and television news for information about the storm, especially in case floods occur and you have to evacuate.

DURING A DOWNPOUR YOU SHOULD:

- Try to remain indoors.
- If you are outside, find dry shelter quickly and use caution while walking; pick your path carefully so you don't slip and fall.
- Don't move around a lot. Downpours make it difficult to see and move. So stay put.
- Avoid walking through water, but if you have to, use a stick to make sure you won't be stepping through anything hazardous. Be extra careful to keep your balance through moving water.

AFTER A DOWNPOUR YOU SHOULD:

- Check your home for floods and leaks.
- Look around outside to see if water has dammed up anywhere. Tell an adult if it has.
- Use caution around drains, especially public drains. Sometimes excess water gets into sewage systems and causes them to overflow. This contaminated water can make you very sick. Don't play in it.

CHANGE IN AVERAGE MONTHLY PRECIPITATION, 2000–2010 (IN INCHES)

- Increase of over 5.0 inches
- Increase of 0.5 to 4.9 inches
- Increase or decrease, < 0.5 inch
- Decrease of -0.5 to 5.0 inches
- Decrease of over 5.1 inches
- No data available

NORTH AMERICA
EUROPE
ASIA
AFRICA
EQUATOR
SOUTH AMERICA
AUSTRALIA
ANTARCTICA

WHEN IT RAINS, IT POURS!

Green/blue indicate places that have become wetter in the world, while yellow/orange/red indicate locations that have become drier.

With intense downpours happening from the United States to India, and with scientists certain that rainfall will increase in the years to come, we may all have to get the right rain gear and plan to spend time indoors, waiting out the rain.

Monsoon season / Meghalaya, India

Drawings showing **raindrops** with a teardrop shape aren't accurate. In the early 20th century, scientists discovered that small falling raindrops were perfectly **round.** When they **grow** to be about 3 millimeters across, they have a hamburger-bun-like shape. Drops **bigger** than 4.5 millimeters break into smaller drops.

Gadgets

HOW DO YOU KNOW HOW MUCH RAIN FELL? Get a rain gauge and find out. These are tube-like gadgets that you can stick in the ground to capture rain and measure how much has fallen. Many of these come with screens to prevent debris from entering at the top, and large numbering so you can easily see how much rain has been collected. You can even make your own rain gauge with a large plastic bottle, scissors, a ruler, and a pen. Have an adult help you cut off the top of the bottle, mark the inches on the bottle (with a water-proof pen) so you can read the numbers, and then leave the bottle out in the rain. You can then record how much it rained.

HOW TO MAKE A RAIN SHELTER

If you get caught outside during a downpour and there aren't any safe and dry shelters close by, building a lean-to may be a good idea. You'll need some basic materials: a poncho or tarp, rope, and sticks. You'll need to find a good location for it—between two trees about six to ten feet (1.8–3 m) apart is best—and you'll want to get an adult to help you put this together.

- First, figure out the direction of the wind. The back of the lean-to should face the wind.
- Next, tie half a line of rope to one end of the "top" corner of your poncho or tarp and the other half to the opposite "top" corner. Tie a small stick a few inches from each end. These act as drip sticks and keep water from leaking inside the lean-to.
- Then tie off the rope ends to each tree, a few feet high.
- Take the loose corners of the material and anchor those to the ground using sharp sticks. The angle from the rope to the ground will keep rain from accumulating on the lean-to. Underneath, you'll stay dry!

RAIN AND WIND SHELTER

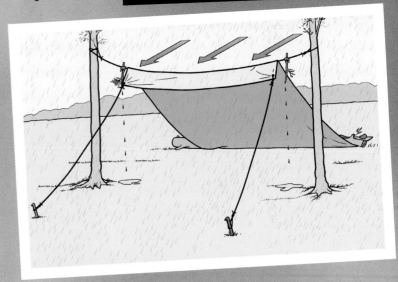

According to climatologist **Heidi Cullen, heavy downpours in the northeastern United States have increased by a whopping 74 percent since the late 1950s.**

FLOODS

[Water surging in and overflowing an area]

WHEN YOU POUR TOO MUCH WATER into a glass or overfill the tub, water spills out. Floods are similar to those spills—just in giant sizes. And just like spills, they happen a lot. In fact, in the United States, they are the most common type of severe weather emergency.

Floods happen any time that water leaks or flows to somewhere it normally isn't located. This can take place in an area around a river or on the coast, because of too much rain, because of snowmelt or ice melt, or because a dam bursts. Actually, it can take place whenever excessive water flows.

River Tawi, Jammu, India / 2010

If it rains a lot, too much water builds up in rivers, lakes, and streams. That extra water can come flooding over the normal edge of the body of water. For example, a storm's winds can push ocean water ashore to cause storm surge flooding. Or if there is a lot more snowmelt or ice melt from the mountains than usual, it can flood the areas below.

There are actually two basic types of floods you should know about. The first is when water rises slowly, and you can see it getting higher and higher or getting into places that it shouldn't go (such as your basement or over the banks of a river). The other type of flood is more dangerous. It's called a "flash flood," and it is when water rises really fast—sometimes so fast that you can't get out of its way.

NATURE'S SIGNAL

Nature has many signals to warn us about a possible flood.

RAIN: If it rains just two inches (5 cm) in less than one hour, there is a good chance floods are on the way. That is because there isn't enough time for the ground to act as a sponge and soak up or absorb all the water being dropped on it.

RISING CREEKS OR STREAMS: If water levels in creeks and streams get high, a flood may occur.

THE COLOR OF WATER: If water in a river turns cloudy or muddy, beware.

NOISE: A "roaring" noise from upstream may mean a flash flood is on its way.

WORMS: Worms wiggle up to the surface before a flood, and you'll see many of them on the ground when waters start to rise.

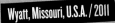

Wyatt, Missouri, U.S.A. / 2011

85

Believe it or not, beavers cause some of these flash floods. Beavers build dams around their homes so they can catch food and to protect themselves from predators such as wolves. They usually build their dams along rivers or creeks to block water from escaping so they can make their own ponds. They stack a lot of tree branches on top of one another to build their dams. While these dams can help control water flow, they can also be a problem when the dams break. When that dam breaks, look out! All that water from the pond comes rushing out and can cause floods somewhere downriver—maybe even where you live.

Floods, no matter how they begin, can bring with them a lot of dangers. The worst flood ever recorded was in China in 1931. It poured rain for a long period of time, snow melted, and all that excess water caused three rivers in China—the Yangtze, Yellow, and Huai Rivers—to overflow and flood the

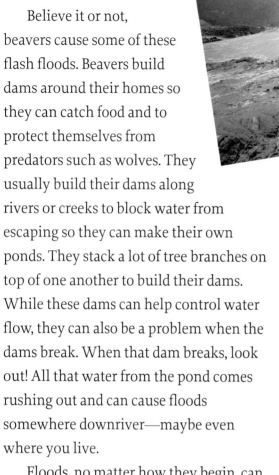

Yemen / 2013

An American beaver dam in Alaska, U.S.A.

BEFORE
A FLOOD YOU SHOULD:

- Know your neighborhood. Investigate how close you are to streams, drainage channels, canyons, and any other low-lying areas that are known to flood.
- Gather contact phone numbers and know where you keep them so you can decide in advance how you will get in touch with family members. Do you have a mobile phone or a walkie-talkie?
- Put together an evacuation plan and share it with everyone in your household. Know what paths and routes you can use to quickly get to a high, dry place.
- Conduct flood drills so you can learn how and how fast you can evacuate.

DURING
A FLOOD YOU SHOULD:

- Never wait for instructions to move; if a real flood is coming, you'll need to evacuate immediately!
- Move to the highest place you can find if you can't get away from a flood in time.
- Move any important items you have to upper floors of your house if it's not too dangerous.
- Never walk through water, and especially avoid moving water. Just six inches (15 cm) of moving water can push you down. If you have to walk in water, walk where the water is still. And remember to never touch or go near electrical equipment if you are standing in water or are wet; you could get electrocuted!

AFTER
A FLOOD YOU SHOULD:

- Return to your home only after officials tell you that it is okay to do so.
- Check around for wild animals, especially snakes. They can get washed into your home with the floodwater.
- Ask an adult if it is all right before you use water to brush your teeth, make food, or even wash your hands. In a flood, the water supply often gets contaminated. That means bad or harmful things get into the water that can make you ill.

Southern Poland / 2010

eXpert Tips

THE U.S. FEDERAL EMERGENCY MANAGEMENT AGENCY says you should be especially prepared for floods after a wildfire. Once trees, plants, and grass get scorched, and because new vegetation hasn't taken root, the land cannot absorb as much water. This means there are fewer places for the water to go. Instead, it keeps moving along the surface and floods begin.

villages around them. Because so many people lived by the rivers, entire communities were washed away. Millions of people were caught in the floods. And the floods didn't go away quickly: They lasted for months. The estimates of the number of people killed in these floods are astounding. It is said that these floods may be responsible for the deaths of up to four million people, from disease, famine, and drowning.

In 2010 in the United States, in parts of the state of Tennessee, nearly two feet (0.6 m) of rain fell over two days. That is a huge amount. All the excess water meant that people had to be evacuated from their homes and had to scramble to find shelter on dry land.

When there is a flood, people can get knocked over and hurt, or they can drown. Most people are injured while they are outside walking or in their cars driving or riding as a passenger. Because of all of these dangers, everyone should become "flood smart."

Gadgets

DID YOU KNOW THERE IS A FAMILY RADIO FREQUENCY that you and your family can tune into to speak with one another? If you have a walkie-talkie, which is like a hand-held radio, you can turn the dial to a specific frequency, almost like tuning in a television channel. If your family members tune in, too, you can speak with them—all at once.

In the United States, the channels are called the Family Radio Service, and the channels, or "bands," are 462 and 467. Having waterproof walkie-talkies preprogrammed to the Family Radio Service can help during a flood. If you can find waterproof walkie-talkies and the kind that also connect to SOS frequencies to let you speak with emergency responders, even better.

Nashville, Tennessee, U.S.A. / 2010

HOW TO BUILD A
BERM

Floods don't have to be huge to cause serious damage. Sometimes floods can come from a garden hose that is accidentally left on or from a neighbor who waters their lawn too much. To stop small floods from leaking into your house, you can build a berm. Build a small mound in front of the place you are trying to protect. Just by using soil, grass, and certain types of plants, you can redirect water flow. But make sure the water doesn't flow somewhere else where it can do damage. Then *you* will be the one creating a flood!

A gardener raised the flower bed, creating a berm, so the planted area wouldn't get flooded.

According to **Jennifer Pipa** of the American Red Cross, **one challenge in helping to rescue people in a flood is that it's hard to know what areas are really affected until the rain has ended.**

A girl walks along a dike in the Netherlands. Dikes hold back the sea, since parts of the country are below sea level.

HURRICANES, TORNADOES & WATER-SPOUTS

People shield
themselves with
umbrellas from the
spray of water during
a storm in Mumbai,
India, 2013.

CHAPTER X

HURRICANES

[When a tropical storm reaches certain wind measurements of 64 knots (74 mph) or greater]

DO YOU KNOW WHAT IT'S LIKE to beat an egg? You whisk it round and round in a bowl until it becomes one color. Hurricane winds whisk ocean waves in a similar way, blowing off their tops to create streaks of white foam across the ocean. Hurricanes are a kind of storm known as tropical cyclones. In the Atlantic Ocean, Caribbean Sea, Gulf of Mexico, and eastern Pacific Ocean, they're called hurricanes. In the western Pacific Ocean, they're called typhoons, and in the southern Pacific and Indian Oceans, they're called cyclones. The strongest ones have winds topping 150 miles an hour (241 kph) and can push more than 20 feet (6 m) of water ashore when they hit land.

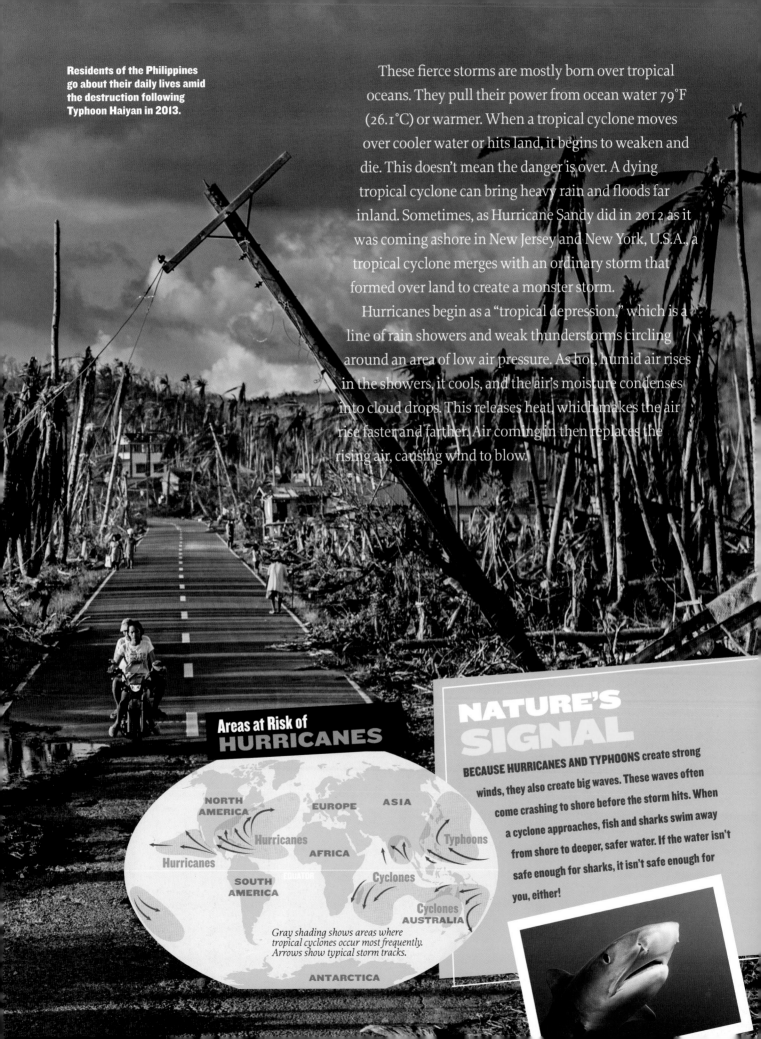

Residents of the Philippines go about their daily lives amid the destruction following Typhoon Haiyan in 2013.

These fierce storms are mostly born over tropical oceans. They pull their power from ocean water 79°F (26.1°C) or warmer. When a tropical cyclone moves over cooler water or hits land, it begins to weaken and die. This doesn't mean the danger is over. A dying tropical cyclone can bring heavy rain and floods far inland. Sometimes, as Hurricane Sandy did in 2012 as it was coming ashore in New Jersey and New York, U.S.A., a tropical cyclone merges with an ordinary storm that formed over land to create a monster storm.

Hurricanes begin as a "tropical depression," which is a line of rain showers and weak thunderstorms circling around an area of low air pressure. As hot, humid air rises in the showers, it cools, and the air's moisture condenses into cloud drops. This releases heat, which makes the air rise faster and farther. Air coming in then replaces the rising air, causing wind to blow.

Areas at Risk of
HURRICANES

NORTH AMERICA
EUROPE
ASIA
Hurricanes
Typhoons
AFRICA
Hurricanes
EQUATOR
Cyclones
SOUTH AMERICA
Cyclones
AUSTRALIA

Gray shading shows areas where tropical cyclones occur most frequently. Arrows show typical storm tracks.

ANTARCTICA

NATURE'S
SIGNAL

BECAUSE HURRICANES AND TYPHOONS create strong winds, they also create big waves. These waves often come crashing to shore before the storm hits. When a cyclone approaches, fish and sharks swim away from shore to deeper, safer water. If the water isn't safe enough for sharks, it isn't safe enough for you, either!

If all the conditions line up, then the clouds grow higher and the winds blow. When they reach 39 miles an hour (63 kph), the depression becomes a tropical storm and forecasters give it a name. When winds reach 74 miles an hour (119 kph), it's a hurricane. When a strong storm is predicted to push high water—known as storm surge—ashore, people in areas that could flood will be urged to evacuate.

As many as 150 tropical cyclones occur around the world each year. While climate scientists don't have a good handle on what a warmer world will mean for tropical cyclones, they have good reasons to think that in the future, we could see fewer of them, but those that occur will be, on average, stronger.

Hurricane Isaac / 2012

Hurricane Sandy / 2012

EVACUATION ROUTE

BEFORE A HURRICANE YOU SHOULD:

- Know the evacuation routes in your neighborhood.
- Check your yard for trees with broken branches. If you see any, let an adult know the branches could fall in a storm.
- Secure your garbage cans and outside furniture—and anything else that could blow away.
- Close all of your windows, storm shutters, blinds, and curtains, and do not go outside.

DURING A HURRICANE YOU SHOULD:

- Leave your house and follow evacuation routes only if instructed to do so by authorities; otherwise, stay indoors where it is safe.
- Do not use your telephone unless it's urgent, in order to free up space for emergency calls.
- Move away from windows and doors. Do not stay in large, open rooms. Huddle in smaller rooms in the center of your home. A closet or hallway on the lowest level can provide safety.
- Do not remain standing. If the storm hits your home, lie on the floor under a table or another sturdy object.

AFTER A HURRICANE YOU SHOULD:

- Listen to weather reports to make sure the storm has passed. There is something called an "eye" of a hurricane when there is calm, and this can trick you into thinking the storm has gone.
- If you have had to evacuate your home, return only when officials say it is safe.
- Check all food for spoilage. Remember: If in doubt, throw it out.

Installing hurricane shutters / Miami, Florida, U.S.A., 2004

eXpert Tips

MAKE A FAMILY COMMUNICATION PLAN.

The U.S. Federal Emergency Management Agency (FEMA) says, "Your family may not be together when disaster strikes, so plan how you will contact one another. Think about how you will communicate in different situations." Create a contact card for each person in your family that lists emergency contact numbers, including your doctor's information, as well as the telephone numbers for people in your family who do not live close by. That way, someone who has not been affected by the storm can be reached. Every family member should keep these cards handy in a wallet, purse, briefcase, or backpack.

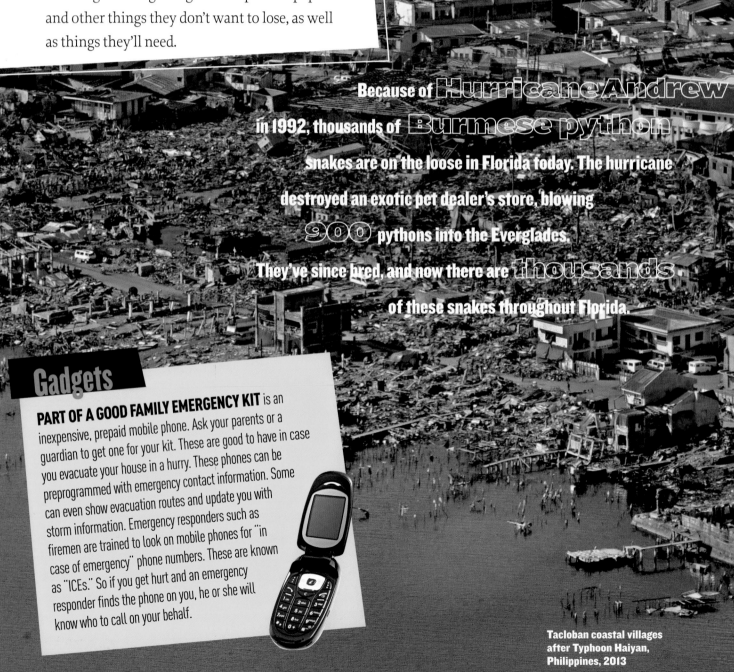

This could mean we will see more storms like Hurricane Sandy or Typhoon Haiyan. When Hurricane Sandy merged with a land-based storm, it killed 159 people and did more than $65 billion in damage. In November 2013, Typhoon Haiyan killed more than 6,000 people in the Philippines.

Those who live anywhere that a hurricane could hit should have plans for evacuation and have a "grab and go" bag with important papers and other things they don't want to lose, as well as things they'll need.

Because of **Hurricane Andrew** in 1992, thousands of **Burmese python** snakes are on the loose in Florida today. The hurricane destroyed an exotic pet dealer's store, blowing **900** pythons into the Everglades. They've since bred, and now there are **thousands** of these snakes throughout Florida.

Gadgets

PART OF A GOOD FAMILY EMERGENCY KIT is an inexpensive, prepaid mobile phone. Ask your parents or a guardian to get one for your kit. These are good to have in case you evacuate your house in a hurry. These phones can be preprogrammed with emergency contact information. Some can even show evacuation routes and update you with storm information. Emergency responders such as firemen are trained to look on mobile phones for "in case of emergency" phone numbers. These are known as "ICEs." So if you get hurt and an emergency responder finds the phone on you, he or she will know who to call on your behalf.

Tacloban coastal villages after Typhoon Haiyan, Philippines, 2013

HOW TO MAKE AN EMERGENCY
CONTACT LIST

This is what a good emergency contact list looks like. Important names, phone numbers, and information that can be helpful to emergency responders should be listed. Also, you should include phone numbers for relatives and close friends who don't live nearby. See if you can make your own.

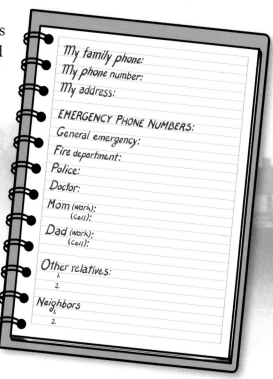

My family phone:
My phone number:
My address:

EMERGENCY PHONE NUMBERS:
General emergency:
Fire department:
Police:
Doctor:
Mom (work):
    (cell):
Dad (work):
    (cell):

Other relatives:
1.
2.
Neighbors
1.
2.

Hurricane Sandy / 2012

TORNADOES

[A quickly spinning column of air that stretches from the ground to the clouds]

IF YOU HAVE EVER SPUN A TOP, you know what a tornado does: It zips around and around and around so fast that it is impossible to count how many turns it takes. For years, what gave tornadoes their twist was a mystery. Since 2010, scientists who get close to tornadoes with Doppler radars on trucks have seen how downdraft winds coming down from high in supercell thunderstorms wrap around air rising into the supercell, giving it the twisting motion that often becomes a tornado. Supercells spin out the strongest tornadoes.

Many windy thunderstorms can be found in a place called Tornado Alley in the United States. This is an area in the middle of the country that extends from Texas to Ohio and includes Iowa, Kansas, South Dakota, and Nebraska. Because warm, moist air comes up from the Gulf of Mexico and crashes into cool air that blows across the country from the Rocky Mountains, it makes the perfect conditions for tornadoes. But a tornado can spring up almost anywhere in the world. They have been spotted on every continent except Antarctica.

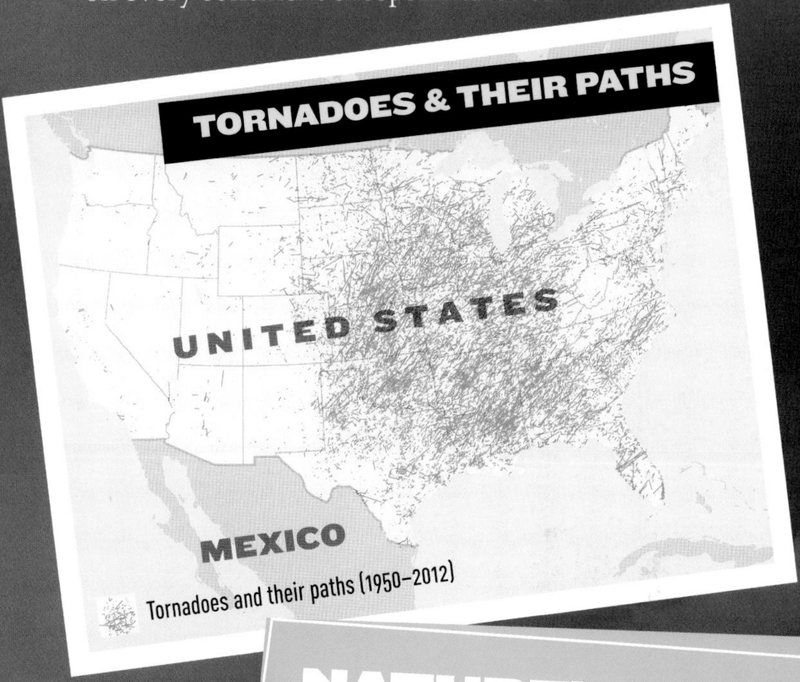

TORNADOES & THEIR PATHS

UNITED STATES

MEXICO

Tornadoes and their paths (1950–2012)

NATURE'S SIGNAL

IF THERE IS A GREENISH TINGE TO THE SKY, tornadoes may be in the area. Your pets can also let you know. They get anxious and act strangely before a tornado. Some dogs howl, cats head for more confined spaces, and birds stop going to feeders.

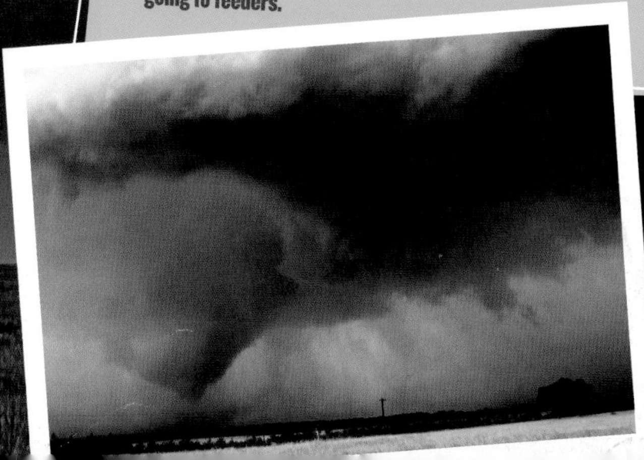

In fact, even though there are more tornadoes in the United States every year than anyplace else, two of the worst tornadoes that ever occurred were in Bangladesh. In 1989, a tornado blew through Bangladesh and injured 12,000 people, killing 600. Twenty years before that, in 1969, another terrible tornado hit what was then called East Pakistan, also injuring thousands of people. It destroyed a lot of buildings, too.

Tornado damage / Bangladesh, 1989

The most damaging tornado in the United States happened in 1925. It is known as the "Tri-State Tornado" because it blew across three states—Missouri, Illinois, and Indiana—and caused an enormous amount of destruction. It trashed homes and schools and leveled entire neighborhoods. Many farms and properties were also destroyed.

Tornadoes are rated on a scale of 0 to 5, according to the amount of damage they did. This scale, the Fujita scale, was invented by Theodore Fujita, a renowned tornado scientist. The scale was updated recently by a team of meteorologists and wind engineers to account for the changing factors that affect the amount of damage done by a tornado.

Residents comb through wreckage in the wake of the Tri-State Tornado, Griffin, Indiana, U.S.A. March 1925.

BEFORE
A TORNADO YOU SHOULD:

● Listen to weather reports for tornado warnings.
● Close all the windows and prepare a safe room in your basement or near the center of your house and away from outer walls and windows.
● Put blankets, pillows, and your family emergency kit (water, food, flashlight, and radio) in the safe room.
● Have an emergency safety plan. In particular, if you live in a trailer or mobile home, make sure you know where to go to evacuate.

DURING
A TORNADO YOU SHOULD:

● Climb under a heavy table if you can and use your arms to cover your head and neck.
● Never attempt to see or chase the tornado. Stay inside until it is gone.
● Try to get into a ditch if you are outside. Then lie down and cover your head with your hands. No matter where you are outdoors, watch out for flying debris.

AFTER
A TORNADO YOU SHOULD:

● Watch where you step—debris is likely all over the ground.
● Listen to public safety officials and follow instructions.
● Continue to monitor tornado reports. Sometimes more than one tornado can whip up in the same place.

eXpert Tips

IF A TORNADO STRIKES, doctors say you should put on a helmet. Almost any type of sturdy helmet will protect your head: a motorcycle helmet, a bicycle helmet, a football helmet, a baseball batting helmet, or even a hard hat like construction workers wear. They say this is important because most people who get injured during tornadoes are hurt by flying objects, such as bricks, pieces of wood, or metal.

The updated scale is called the Enhanced Fujita (EF) scale. An EF0 tornado has three-second gust speeds of less than 86 miles an hour (138 kph) and results in some damage to chimneys, tree branches, and shrubs. An EF5 tornado has three-second gust speeds of over 200 miles an hour (322 kph). That can be faster than a Formula One race car! An EF5 tornado can cause incredible damage, such as ripping houses off their foundations and sending vehicles flying through the air. Very few tornadoes are rated EF5.

Knowing what to do if you spot a tornado is important. It can mean the difference between staying safe and getting hurt.

With winds that travel **superfast,** it should be no surprise that tornadoes can **carry** some very large, and unexpected things away ... such as **COWS!**

Gadgets

AS PART OF YOUR TORNADO EMERGENCY KIT, include a whistle. But not just any whistle; get a special storm whistle. These are louder than the whistle you might use on the soccer field or to start a race. They're also waterproof and windproof. If you need help, get stuck or trapped, or see danger coming (such as a tornado!), a whistle can help.

Washington, Illinois, U.S.A. / 2013

HOW TO POSTION YOUR BODY WHEN A
TORNADO HITS

Of course you should **FIND A SAFE PLACE** to wait out a tornado. But you should also **GET INTO THE RIGHT POSITION.** That means facing an inside wall, crouching with your knees and elbows on the ground, and placing your hands over the back of your head.

BE EARTH FRIENDLY!

TRY THIS ENERGY-REDUCING TIP! When washing your clothes, use cold water instead of hot.

WATER-SPOUTS

[A rotating column of air over water]

A WATERSPOUT IS ONE OF THE coolest-looking things you might ever see. It's like the water coming out of a faucet—without the faucet! A stream of water spins round and round and appears to float on its own.

Imagine taking a bucket of water and tossing the water out into the air. Then imagine that the water gets whipped up by the wind and starts to spin around like a tornado. That's exactly what a waterspout looks like—except some waterspouts rise up from the ocean or a lake. They mostly happen over warm water. The spinning winds of waterspouts look just like a tornado, but something different is happening.

There are two types of waterspouts. The first type are "tornadic" waterspouts. These begin as tornadoes on land and then droplets condense inside the funnel to make them become waterspouts. These waterspouts bring their land baggage, such as thunder and lightning, with them and are stronger than the more common "fair weather" waterspouts, which rise into clouds. Fair weather waterspouts begin on the surface of water and climb high into the sky. Water gets lifted from the surface of the ocean or a lake by wind and spins higher into the air. Its funnel often looks hollow, but it is filled with spray and high winds. This spray can rise several hundred feet or more (taller than many buildings) and can create a train of waves in its wake. Waterspouts do most of their damage to places along a coastline when they slam ashore.

NATURE'S SIGNAL

WHEN A FAIR WEATHER WATERSPOUT IS FORMING, a dark spot occurs on the surface of the water. Water then starts to swirl, and the dark spot is surrounded by a larger, darker area of water. After that, a spiral pattern of light-and-dark-colored water forms in bands—sort of like a ripple on a pond. A swirling ring of sea spray, called a cascade, then begins. This lifts the water from the surface and spins it higher into the air. After that, the waterspout will take shape.

They usually don't last a long time—typically around 20 minutes. Still, waterspouts can be really dangerous. They have overturned boats, damaged large ships, and even killed people.

In ancient times, people really didn't know what waterspouts were. They believed waterspouts were streams of water pouring from the sky as if by magic or a work of the gods. But we now know that isn't true.

Throughout history, sailors have reported seeing waterspouts. In fact, there was one report of a waterspout that started off the coast of Italy in 1456.

Double waterspouts / Lake Michigan, U.S.A., 2013

Waterspouts observed in the Mediterranean, near Sicily, Italy, 1827

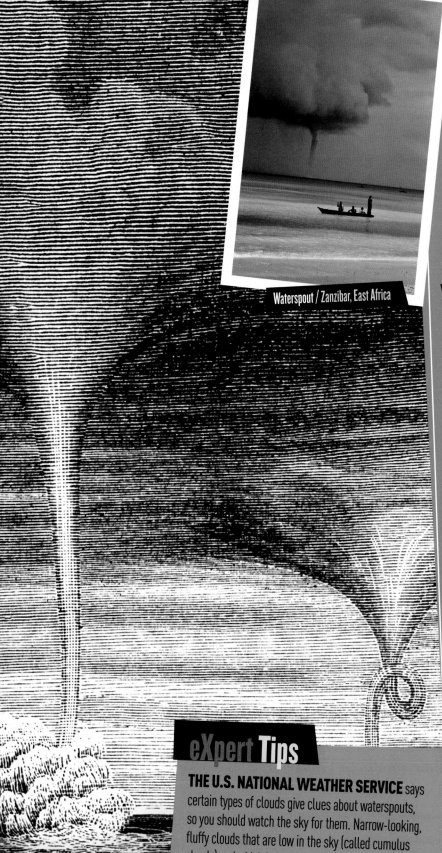

Waterspout / Zanzibar, East Africa

BEFORE
A WATERSPOUT YOU SHOULD:

● Check weather forecasts for storms, especially if you are near warm water.
● Look for dark, disk-shaped-patches on surface waters. These can be warning signs.
● If you are in a boat, have a plan for how you will quickly get to shore.
● Even if you are onshore, you should take the same precautions that you would with a tornado, because waterspouts can move onto land and become a tornado. Have a go-to shelter area ready, an evacuation route ready, and an emergency kit on hand.

DURING
A WATERSPOUT YOU SHOULD:

● Get to your safe room if you are at home.
● If you are in a boat, tell whoever is steering to immediately head at a 90-degree angle from the direction the waterspout is moving. So if a waterspout is heading directly at your boat, the boat should head sharply to the right or left.
● Remember: **Never** chase a waterspout.

AFTER
A WATERSPOUT YOU SHOULD:

● If you are on a boat, head for shore and get to safe, dry ground as far inland as possible.
● Keep listening to weather reports in case there are more waterspouts in the area and in your path.
● Be on the lookout for any piles of debris or damaged areas onshore.

eXpert Tips

THE U.S. NATIONAL WEATHER SERVICE says certain types of clouds give clues about waterspouts, so you should watch the sky for them. Narrow-looking, fluffy clouds that are low in the sky (called cumulus clouds) and which have dark, flat bottoms may be a sign of waterspouts in the making. During summertime, if there are light winds blowing, you should look for waterspouts underneath these types of clouds. Also, thunderstorms produce waterspouts, so beware if these storms are predicted or are in the area.

More recently, in 2013, two boaters chased waterspouts off the coast of Florida, U.S.A. Their boat nearly flipped over. They filmed their adventure and posted the video on the Internet. Chasing the waterspout was a stupid and dangerous thing to do, and they said they would never do it again.

Whether you live near the water or only sometimes visit a local lake, knowing what weather can occur is the first step toward staying safe. Always be aware of your surroundings and be sure to check the weather report before you plan an outing.

Waterspouts can make it rain frogs and fish. Just as land tornadoes can lift animals (like cows) and heavy objects off the ground, waterspouts can lift marine animals into the air. The winds from a waterspout are powerful enough to suck up a school of fish in one place and drop them like rain somewhere else.

Gadgets

IF YOU GO BOATING OFTEN OR LIVE BY A COAST, you may want to ask an adult to get you a marine radio. These allow you to listen to and speak on all marine channels so you can hear what ships' captains are saying. Many of these radios come equipped with hazardous weather alerts. If a waterspout is in the area, marine authorities will usually send out a warning signal.

CONCLUSION
& FURTHER READING

You can do something about the weather! If there is one thing that you should remember from this book, it is to prepare.

You can read up and know what to expect and what to do when extreme weather hits (by studying this book), or you can wear the right type of clothing, or you can keep that emergency kit handy—all of these actions, and more, will help to keep you safe.

Staying safe is, of course, what this book is about. Along with safety, you hopefully will have learned some fun and interesting facts about our planet and how the forces of nature work to create weather.

Learning how to do your part so weather doesn't get worse is important, too. Don't stray off marked paths and kick up dirt that can turn into a sandstorm. Turn off the lights so you don't waste electricity, contribute to a blackout, or more important, put more pollution in the air that can lead to global warming and climate change. To create more electricity, we have to pollute the air. When we use clean energy and use less electricity, there's less pollution. These little steps can go a long way—just imagine if everyone on the planet followed these few small directions.

Of course, there's lots more you can do:

Search the Internet to find information about the weather and what you can do now and for the future to make things better and safer.

The Federal Emergency Management Agency's website for kids, *http://www.ready.gov/kids,* is a good place to start. Or check out the American Red Cross's website for kids, *http://www.redcross.org/prepare/location/home-family/children.*

There are apps *(http://www.kidweatherapp.com)* and games (http://www.weatherwizkids.com/weather-games.htm), too!

Of course, National Geographic *(http://kids.nationalgeographic.com)* has tons of fun and interesting videos, photos, and even more books on weather that you should check out.

Taking action at school and in your community are also good ways to get others involved, or to teach them to be more aware of the weather.

The future of weather and our climate is really up to us. Working together, we have the opportunity to change the world and make it safer for everybody. Just by reading this book, you've already learned some cool things, right? Why not learn more? Why not do more? Start now!

INDEX

Because of drought, reservoirs—such as this one in California, U.S.A., 2014—have low water levels.

PHOTO CREDITS